Home
Style
Teaching

2374

Books by Raymond and Dorothy Moore

Home-Spun Schools
Home-Grown Kids
Better Late than Early
School Can Wait
Home-Made Health
Home-Style Teaching

Home Style Teaching

A Handbook for Parents and Teachers

Raymond & Dorothy Moore

WITH DENNIS MOORE, M.A.,
KATHLEEN KORDENBROCK, A.B., AND JOLENE OSWALD, PH.D.

WORD PUBLISHING
Dallas · London · Sydney · Singapore

*To parents and teachers
who love their children enough
to put them first*

All Scripture quotations, unless otherwise noted, are from the King James Version of the Bible.

Library of Congress Cataloging in Publication Data

Moore, Raymond S.
  Home-style teaching.
  Includes bibliographical references.
  1. Domestic education. 2. Home and school.
3. Teaching. I. Moore, Dorothy N. II. Title.
LC37.M67 1984   649'.68   84–5127
ISBN 0–8499–3132–0

Printed in the United States of America

  1 2 3 9 FG 9 8 7 6 5 4 3

CONTENTS

Foreword

OUR IMPRESSIONS about parents as teachers have undergone a dramatic and favorable shift. For years families were led to believe that they did not have the necessary ability to help children learn. This view was reinforced by the government in 1965 with the beginning of Head Start, a massive early childhood program based on the premise that some children needed rescue from family influence. Later, when research studies confirmed that parents have more impact on the self-concept and language development of children than anyone else, our federal government changed its course. The emphasis on trying to compensate for parents' lack of training has been replaced by efforts to support parent development.

Consider the unique possibilities of parent influence. The ideal of individualized instruction can routinely take place in the home. Indeed, the family has the most desirable teacher-pupil ratio at a time in life when it counts the most. Parents are generally the only teachers a child has during the period of most rapid growth. Certainly they are the child's only continuous source of guidance throughout the growing up years. Because boys and girls closely identify with parents, mothers and fathers have a great opportunity to convey values and develop communication skills. Together these are sufficient reasons for helping parents improve themselves as teachers.

7

Unfortunately, some parents do not make the most of their chance for influence. Like the children they raise, these adults lack confidence in themselves and sincerely believe they should limit instruction at home so as to not interfere with the effort of the school faculty. Unless parents feel capable of providing a learning environment, they are likely to withdraw from teaching and expect professionals to become primarily responsible for child-rearing. When this attitude is taken, children lose a potentially valuable source of learning. In addition, because boys and girls look up mainly to those who help them adapt and grow, non-teaching parents forfeit the respect they desire and deserve.

Whether your intention is to conduct a school at home or augment the instruction that children receive elsewhere, this book will be a valuable resource. By taking advantage of the collective insights provided by the authors, you can adopt more reasonable child-rearing expectations; acquire better methods for teaching and guidance; develop greater self-confidence as an educator; and experience more satisfaction in day-to-day relationships with your sons and daughters.

ROBERT D. STROM, Ph.D.
Director, Office of Parent Development International
College of Education, Arizona State University

Why This Book Was Written for Both Parents and Teachers

Home-Style Teaching is a simplified, research-based handbook designed for both parents and professional teachers and for student teachers who are worried about becoming professionals. The parents may be either home-schoolers or those who wish to help their children who are troubled by school or failing. This book sets out to make clear what education should really be and to make the art and science of teaching as understandable, successful, and thrilling as it *can* be. This may not be for you. We do not say that all parents should home-school their children. Some will not be suited for this task, psychologically or physically or financially. We do say that most normal parents can do it very well, even though the great majority have doubts about their abilities.

With this book, we hope to take parents and teachers by the hand and lead them to courage and wisdom in one of the greatest of all professions. We hope to bring bright new understanding, even to those who have been through university education courses—which we admit to directing for many years. We base our conclusions not only on long and varied experience—but also on the work of our research teams at Stanford,[1] University of Colorado Medical School,[2] and in Michigan.[3]

Home-Style Teaching applies to the regular school as well as to the home. It complements our line of research-based parent-education books, designed to show why and how to educate your children, and the way many families are doing it—*Better Late Than Early, School Can Wait, Home-Grown Kids,* and *Home-Spun Schools.*[4]

This book is a team-teaching effort by five professionals who have taught around the world: developmental psychologist *father,* who has taught and administered at all levels; reading specialist *mother,* whom the family recognizes as their master teacher; developmental psychologist *son,* who has taught at elementary and college levels and is our lead researcher; early-childhood specialist *daughter* from the Sacramento, California, public schools, on leave to mother two young sons; and our dear friend and deeply respected teacher of teachers, Dr. Jolene Oswald of Michigan's Spring Arbor College.

Father has been dean of teacher education in several colleges and universities. His research and teaching associations have ranged from the University of Southern California, Stanford, Southern Illinois University, and the University of Chicago, to Japan and the Philippines and the United States Office of Education. He has directed the Hewitt Research Foundation for twenty years. Both *father* and *mother* are members of the faculty of the University of Nevada's National College of Juvenile and Family Court Judges. And *father* and *mother* and *son* are research associates of the Office of Parent Development International at Arizona State University. You will read more about Dorothy Moore in her chapter on reading.

When "I" is used herein, it will usually be *father,* the lead author, but the manuscript is the product of all five and had to pass muster with a corps of parents, teachers, and teachers of teachers.

In this book you will find some repetition. We have planted it deliberately (and we hope discreetly), in our effort to stress certain important techniques, some of which teachers do not commonly practice or do not understand. These methods may be considered the secrets of great teaching, the greatest of which is most often done by parents who think enough of their children to give them the best, no matter the risk or cost. And this "best" is usually themselves—their warm responses, their examples, their encouragement, and their inspiration. We will verify and show why and how parents are still potentially the world's greatest teachers—academically as well as behaviorally—and why parental schooling is a far richer educational investment than institutionalizing young children before they can possibly be ready.

Remember, we think not only of you parents who have decided on complete school programs at home, but fondly also of you teachers in schools—where sometimes things don't go too well. And we also consider the home school as a laboratory for all education. Thus, learning materials such as our *Math-It, Winston Grammar Game,* self-teaching *Moore-McGuffey Readers,* and character-development tape stories[5] have been lauded as miracle workers for parents whose troubled children are already in school and whom the parents can help at home. They not only help the child, but also bring the family closer together.

I. Becoming a Good Teacher

1. Some TLC (Tender, Loving Care) Hints for a New Teacher from an Old Classroom Hack

THERE WERE TIMES in my teacher-education courses in college when I wished the teachers would put down their recipe—one, two, three, four, with no flourishes—just to get me into the action. Their courses did little to help my confidence as a student teacher, and I became more apprehensive as graduation neared. To make matters worse, my fiancée was already a highly successful teacher in the Whittier, California, public schools, and had just been appointed the reading specialist for her school district. It did encourage me somewhat to get an *A* in student teaching, but my college was not yet accredited for offering state credentials. I had to look forward to earning a teaching certificate by Los Angeles County examination. I was later amazed that I passed decently, and although I had been teaching part-time for five years, I was scared of my first full-time teaching job.

So go the apprehensions of new teachers, and also of parents who are planning to teach their own for the first time. This is especially true when the state is breathing hotly down their necks. But there the similarity ends. It was another fifteen years before I had confidence in my teaching. I had been a college professor, graduate dean, and college president, when some of my former student teachers came to honor me.

I believe that most teachers need years to develop a confidence that is more than bravado. Yet we find that deeply convicted

15

home-schooling parents—most of whom are afraid at first—actually settle into confident teaching within a few weeks or months. Their instincts, their one-to-one relationship with their "students," and the positive changes in their children in contrast to others gives early comfort that few professionals are privileged to experience. And parents who plan well ahead, sometimes for years, have the easiest time of all. Educators who read this chapter (and hopefully, parents, too) will soon sense that it was written by someone who has been out there with them and, in most cases, before them.

You may safely assume that few professional teachers understand the basic principles of great education. Most teachers were taught that the most important learning comes from books, and most teach as they were taught. They have never learned—as this book tells elsewhere—that the greatest teaching involves many loving and thoughtful one-to-one responses, inspiring and encouraging adult examples, and much freedom to explore.

At first this may seem overly simplistic or old-fashioned, but be patient and merciful in your judgment. Simple ideas and methods are usually the most effective, and old-fashioned items often wear well. I had the good fortune of sitting at the feet of many great old teachers and to learn, as did Ralph Waldo Emerson, that the years teach much which the days never know. The techniques we talk about here have been proven again and again through generations in both home and school. There are repetitions, but it often takes such emphases to jolt us from the tedium and tradition which have buried much of education in Greco-Roman graves, along with their societies that went down before ours. It takes a loud voice to raise from the dead.

Teaching is inspiring a student rather than filling him with facts. It is responding to him rather than demanding of him. It is motivating him to explore on his own rather than controlling his explorations. It is inducing him to think, rather than repeating others' thoughts. Teaching is leading others to be like you—and more. It is finding lessons in everything you see, hear, smell, taste, and touch, and bringing them together to give deeper meaning and fulfillment to life.

The order of the following hints may leave something to be desired, but we hope that the reemergence of old truths in new contexts will strengthen them in your mind, whether you are teaching at home or in an institution.

1. *Organization.* Although you do not have to become highly formalized, do your best to plan systematically. Have a place for everything and teach both your students and yourself to keep everything in its place. Keep small pieces of note paper in your shirt or apron pocket. Make a daily list of things to do. At the end of the day, make a new list for tomorrow, carrying forward the things undone. Keep a brief daily journal of your school activities, and have your students do the same. This is a great motivator for organization and can be a lot of fun now and later. At home or at school, the examples of your own self-discipline will teach more than you can by words. Carefully make your schedule to serve you—and follow it. But if something more worthwhile comes up, don't be a slave to your schedule.

2. *Discipline and Self-Control.* Discipline is the art of making disciples, and a great leader must first learn to be a good follower. Such sound discipline will come as a product of self-control, which is best developed by focusing on the needs of others. This highest type of discipline can never be built in a selfish individual or society. Self-discipline and self-respect are best found through service and concern for our neighbors. The student—and the teacher—who learns this will evoke a more productive society.

3. *Relaxation.* If you are a warm, responsive person, you will likely be a good teacher. Relax, at least enough to be a loving person rather than a tense beast. No teacher is perfect, but all good teachers see their students as persons with lives filled with acceptance and worthwhile accomplishments. Wrap your heart around them. It will help you forget yourself.

4. *Imagination and Leadership.* Lead your students. See yourself as a shepherd, guiding, but not as a sheep dog, barking at your "lambs." See a lesson in their every question, an illustration in everything touched by your life and those of your children. Give wide rein to your imagination.

5. *Physical Tone.* Keep slim, active, and physically fit. Don't

get out of condition. Eat to live. Don't live to eat—and drink. Get plenty of constructive exercise. Get your rest, for the sake of your own patience. The hours before midnight are at least twice as valuable for sleep as the early morning hours. And, for study, the hours before breakfast are three to five times as valuable as the time after supper.

6. *Systems View.* See your children as important people in building their school, their community, and their nation. Help them gain the broad view of being producers and servers rather than always being served.

7. *Course of Study.* If it isn't chosen for you, select your curriculum carefully. Take good counsel and use your imagination. Don't let the course of study panic you. Look it over in relation to each subject or activity. Then set your goals accordingly and work toward them systematically, following the schedules you set.

8. *The Teacher-Classroom Manager.* You do not have to know everything. You cannot. Many children know more than their teachers about many things. The teacher's main business is to stimulate imagination and encourage inquiry, not to fill heads with facts as one would glasses from a pitcher. Rather, you are the classroom manager, at school or at home. You know where you and your students can find needed information. Be constantly on the lookout for promising new sources and techniques. Teach what you can yourself. But, for much of your task, help your students become specialists in areas that they especially like, and let them help you teach. They can often teach more effectively than you. In fact, their education is incomplete if they are not imparting as they learn.

9. *Use of Students as Teachers.* There may be a wide variety of abilities in your home or classroom. Some students will be very good in math, for example, but poor in reading. Few will really lag in everything. Use the stronger to help the weaker and the older to help the younger. Children will often be able to teach one thing but need help in another. A good classroom manager allows for such arrangements.

10. *Diagnosis.* If a child does seem "slow," be suspicious first

of his health, sight, hearing, home problems, boredom, burnout, and so forth. Here is where TLC takes over and makes you a great teacher.

11. *Teacher-Learner.* Don't hesitate to seek help—from a fellow teacher, homemaker, physician, or principal. Study the techniques of other effective parents and teachers.

12. *Prompt Record-Keeping.* Keep up-to-date reports—daily or periodic—including a brief daily journal or diary. This is a must for good relationships with the principal and the school system or for your home school's accounting to the state. Procrastination is deadly in teaching.

13. *Dependability in Students.* Insist that your students also keep up to date. You must educate them to be prompt and dependable. This is far more important than getting *A*'s or *B*'s in language or math. Give them more projects than workbooks—assignments that excite them and stretch their minds. Check on their projects in stages, to see that they are learning as they go, whether they are making a bas-relief map out of flour and salt and water and colored with available paints, fashioning a steam engine from a can, or building a tractor from a thread spool, a match stick, and a rubber band.

14. *Motivation: Knowing the Individual.* Search out early the abilities and interests of each child at home or at school. Tests and records already on hand will often help you. Then use these abilities and interests as gateways to meaningful production and sound rapport. Are your children mechanically inclined? Do they have special language backgrounds? Are they musical? Interested in scientific observation? When you appeal to their personal needs and skills, you are developing powerful intrinsic motivation from needs within them instead of pressures or threats imposed from outside.

15. *Building Mutual Respect.* Challenge your students. Don't plead, but see that they work! It is not your primary business to amuse. They will respect you more if you let them know you have confidence in them. Trust begets trust. *Expect top effort.* Point them toward leadership in their communities, to development of sound values in society and in their professions, to build-

ing of strong manhood and womanhood to the glory of their nation and their God.

16. *Reading Resources.* Provide ample high-order reading resources that meet the personal needs of your students on mental, physical, vocational, social, and inspirational levels. But be sure of the quality of this material.[1] If you are teaching in an institution, utilize parent committees to help your choices. If you are in a home school, talk with other parents and your pastor. You will find that libraries and families usually cooperate freely. In home schools, a range of good books—your own or from libraries—is also a great supplement to your work and stimulates many responses.

17. *Vocational Eye-Openers.* Involve parents or other qualified people from time to time—physicians, ministers, lawyers, nurses, and so on—to tell about their professions and to inspire. Give students a chance to question. However, if you are in school, don't allow guests to talk too long or to crowd recesses. If at home, don't let unexpected visitors or your telephone mold your day.

18. *Delegate and Check.* Check frequently on performance through short tests and other evaluation techniques. Utilize students to help in grading (perhaps using numbers instead of names to identify papers, to protect privacy). Exchange papers in a variety of ways, and while you are reading the answers, demand absolute attention in correcting the tests.

19. *Paper Work.* Don't get bogged down with loads of papers at night. Before leaving school for the day, most of your work should be completed for that day and your schedule arranged for the next. *Organization* and using students to help are keys here. If you are teaching at home, don't put such things off. You can usually go over your students' papers in class.

20. *Thoroughness.* Insist on high standards. Every paper you require should be corrected—by you or the students. *Be sure every student goes over his marked paper and corrects everything.* Perfection should be your goal. You need not pressure the students, but you can keep that carrot well out in front so as to keep them on the track.

21. *Cooperative Teaching.* Utilize students in all classroom pro-

jects and lesson preparations. Those who work with you will not work against you! This is *constructive* discipline. Preventive discipline (seeing and preventing a "situation" before it fully develops) is much better than remedial action. Learn *with* your students. Even though in some subjects they will know more than you, lead them—in love. They are the leaders of tomorrow. And *you* will need *them* one day! As a college president, I have had students turn up years later on my board. More than once my former students have had a part in hiring me. And your children may one day be taking care of you!

22. *Heart to Heart.* On the first day of school, and periodically thereafter, drop everything and have a candid talk. Let your students know that everyone is expected to learn certain skills in order to be able to face life. Reading, math, spelling, good speech, writing, and sound handling of money are survival skills. Not everyone in the class will necessarily be required to perform precisely the same assignments, for some have already acquired this knowledge or certain skills. When you are convinced that a student knows a subject thoroughly, you will not dog him with more assignments nor try to make him regurgitate mental food he has already digested. Great education calls for few workbooks.

23. *Honor System.* If possible, have some kind of student-administered honor system under your guidance. In any event, remind the class early in the year that not only will cheating not be tolerated, but also that you expect to conduct the class in such a fair manner that it will not be considered necessary to cheat. Welcome their coming to you if they have problems, yet avoid encouraging unnecessary complaints or harassment. A high level of motivation to happy service and sound citizenship will give you strength.

24. *Appreciation.* Be long on encouragement, even though it may sometimes be hard to give. Walk tall and breathe confidence because you have it. Compliment frequently—publicly, if merited, or privately when that seems advisable. Be fair with all and distribute your attention as evenly as possible. Ensure that every child has a daily success experience even if *you* have to arrange it.

25. *Consistency.* The teacher who is consistent, even if his or

her habits are not perfect, tends to give the students greater security and comes across as better organized. Consistency is a teacher's precious jewel.

26. *Supervised Study.* Make homework, if any, creative and appropriate to a student's ability.[2] Assign it on a project basis, giving time over days or weeks, but checking systematically and explicitly on progress. One student may have a scientific project; another may put together a telegraph set as did early railroaders. Others may write an article or a song, make paper or flour-and-salt dough models for a teaching unit, or help decorate a house or the schoolroom. In other words, make homework creative. Concede to rote assignments only when such remedial work is absolutely necessary, but never let it simply become "busy work" (to keep the children occupied so that they will not get in the parents' hair). One of the best homework projects is keeping a daily journal. This is especially fruitful for home schools. It demonstrates system, helps in the ability to write, and is an excellent record.

28. *Involvement.* Relate projects to your classroom work as a whole, insofar as possible. For example, measuring things or making items and selling them are great for arithmetic, whether in the kitchen or classroom or garage. Have your children report in detail to you or to the entire class, as indicated. Occasionally have a school fair or open house for parents where the results of your students' work can be seen.

29. *Initiative.* Encourage students to seek professional help on their own. For example, watch flower arranging at a local florist, take the class to a nearby printer or publisher, get some help on establishing an honor system by visiting a lawyer. Let two or more youngsters work together if the combination is compatible.

30. *Balance.* Provide a balanced program of work and study. This offsets mental strain, develops character, and builds initiative, industry, responsibility. Have every student in class assigned one or more daily/weekly responsibilities in the home on which he will report and—if you are in a regular classroom—on which you will work with his parents in developing promptness, respect,

cleanliness, dependability, and so on. In such a case, if the student does not have home cooperation, give him a job with you at school. But do not make a single exception. It must be a case of "everybody's doing it," either at home or school. And give your child (or children) a grade, in consultation with the parents. For home schools, this privilege of working together freely is the cream.

31. *Home Visits.* If practicable, visit every home as early as possible and at least once or twice during the year. It takes time, but it is worth it. Before your first visit, know your student, including his past record. But visit to learn about him, not necessarily (or only) to teach his parents. Visit again later in the year. *Don't show partiality to any parent or home.* If you are home-schooling, involve your child in making things for others—bread, cookies, simple toys or other crafts—and taking them to those who are needy or ill, or to neighbors whom you would like to befriend, especially if they need to be more understanding of home-schooling.

32. *Nobility.* While we cannot guarantee perfect results, we must help every child to excel in something, and we must build self-worth. It will then be easier to help him become honest, dependable, orderly, prompt, courteous, and otherwise develop refinement and the balanced character which a sound society requires. We repeat: lead and encourage your students in doing good for others. They will dignify what you dignify: projects for neighbors, for the feeble or ill, or for the community.

33. *Practical Instruction.* Don't put down book learning, but don't be its slave either. Recognize its importance, but show its application to worthwhile projects—a garden for science; class paper, diary, or personal experience as subjects for short creative writing exercises; model villages from salt dough for bas-relief maps for social studies, and for art; charts, budgets, or family spending guides for math, and so on.

34. *Personalized Projects.* Relate student projects to home, church, or community whenever possible. In regular schools, this brings involvement and support for your teaching program. For example, plan a school or class garden. Each child can have

his own little section. All will delight in taking home some vegetables or flowers. Students might sell vegetables and use the money for a class, school, or home purpose. Sound gardening advice may be secured from experienced people in your area. Vegetable and flower seedlings can even be raised in classrooms in galvanized metal trays which can easily be made by local metal tradesmen. In home schools, form your own family corporation (either "dummy" or real) and run a cottage industry.

35. *Sense of Humor.* You may expect problems, but don't invite them! Seek sound counsel. Be patient and teachable. In schools, avoid practical jokes and the entrance by students into your personal affairs—remarks about your boyfriend, girlfriend, or family, for example. These and other familiarities must not be permitted. Never allow students to call you by your first name. On the other hand, *a sense of humor is vital. Love is the key,* for it helps you see yourself through your students' eyes and know how to distinguish between the bad and the good.

36. *Gossip and Confidences.* Never share random information that would not bear repeating in the presence of the one who is being discussed. In a professional matter, such as discipline, deal only with those who are, or should be, ethically concerned. To violate a confidence, in classroom, office, or home, is one of the most serious and undermining breaches of ethics. We repeat, *never violate* a confidence, not even to another teacher or your roommate or spouse. Make this an absolute habit. Say only good things about others or keep quiet, unless there is a serious problem, and then act in this order: (1) go alone to the student or other person involved; (2) take someone else along; (3) finally, consult parents, pastor, or others, depending on the nature of the problem. Be a peacemaker. The only possible exception should be when a felony or life-or-death situation is at stake.

37. *Poise.* As a teacher, you are thrust into a position of prominence in the community. Neither dodge the spotlight nor seek it; just be worthy of the esteem of all. Parents and others will judge you, but you are not to judge them. Your wisdom and character, your common sense and dedication, will be a constant

witness. Stand tall. Make the Golden Rule your constant guide.

38. *Authority-Responsibility.* In school and home, the job of building children, experience by experience, so that they can take responsibility for the authority they gradually demand, requires a certain risk on the part of the teacher and the parent. For example, permitting a child to take out the family car, before he can be held financially responsible for an accident, is an experience that faces nearly every Western parent. Responsibility must always be the basis for authority. Yet the judgment of the youth must be ventured and respected or he will never develop discernment. Our principal job, then, is to educate not only for knowledge and skill, but also for wisdom and sound judgment. This is your greatest glory. You must emphasize responsibility as the foundation for authority, and practical work as a builder of self-worth.

39. *Training and Education.* Training is often mistaken for education. The good teacher will ever be aware of the differences and will discover both the economies of *training* and the challenges to the highest goals in *education.* Training does not require much reasoning, e.g., as in learning the *ABC*'s or how to type. Education is effective only in proportion to its use of reasoning and judgment. Training is an expedient that appeals to instincts and coordination. Education builds on principle and appeals to reason for discovering the basic *whys* of life. Training is necessary for animals and for human responses that place a low requirement on reason, as with little children or the severely retarded. Education develops judgment, wisdom, and creative effort which animals cannot know. The newborn baby, who is almost totally without reason, and must be trained, we hope will gradually become a consistently thoughtful person by age eight to twelve and thus fully educable. Teaching reaches its highest point when it prepares the human mind and heart for creative service for others—living by the Golden Rule, "in honour preferring one another." [3]

40. *Faith.* America was founded upon a deep trust in God. Many teachers find unusual strength and stability here. In

referring to his students, one teacher recently said, "Every time I lead the Pledge of Allegiance to my country, I sense that my every student is a child of God." Here is a teacher who has his values straight and thus seldom needs to worry about his ability to teach.

2. How You Develop Confidence as a Great Teacher

IN 1981, BRENDA LEWIS, a harassed Indiana mother, addressed a letter to psychologist James Dobson of the popular radiocast "Focus on the Family." It was 11:15 P.M., nearly seventeen hours after her day had begun.

"It's been one of those days!" the troubled woman wrote. "Last Saturday, I listened to the tape on WBCL radio in Fort Wayne with Raymond Moore about *Home-Grown Kids.* I feel he is in some areas out of touch with reality. It seems to me he is unable to imagine a woman's being a good mother and working.

"As you can guess, I am a career mother. I also love my kids and husband. I stayed home until my youngest son was nearly five years old. After the program Saturday, I felt hurt and bewildered as a . . . mother."

She went on to describe the high stress level of her job as a professional woman, continuing more in confession than in protest: "I must be at work by 9:00 A.M. and never leave the office until at least 5:30 P.M. I then come home to fix dinner, do the mountain of laundry, straighten up the house, and help my children and husband with their needs. I am exhausted . . . *but* I am bored when I stay home, and under pressure to work to help ease the financial strain. . . . I am praying that people like Raymond Moore will understand that women like myself are good moms even without breast feeding and teaching our kids at home. . . ."

When Dr. Dobson forwarded Brenda's letter to us, we wrote her a love letter and let her in on an apparently closely held secret: the Moores don't preach that working mothers don't love their kids.

A year passed in the life of our heroine.

In 1982, now more desperate than hurt, she got in touch with us directly. She telephoned that her eight-year-old boy had developed serious problems in a local church school. He was "showing signs of withdrawing from reality." She and her husband were advised by local school officials to take him to a psychiatrist at $70 per hour. When he was in first grade, his teacher had let the word drop that Brenda's little boy should really not be in school, so they had waited before starting him again. But now he had a mental block about reading. "The funny thing about it," his mother recalled later, "was that when he left school for summer vacation he seemed to act like a normal child again."

Another year passed.

The other day our heroine called us again, this time excited, enthusiastic, ecstatic. She could not stop talking, and it was a delightful report. Brenda had chosen to stay home with her children "until they are mature." She told us that the psychiatrist couldn't get over her son's "remarkable improvement," and said that he didn't need to come back any more, "except perhaps a visit every three months or so just to see how he is doing."

She quit her office job long ago and is "making out just fine, now working from our home here as a management consultant." In closing, she added that she is thoroughly and positively sold on motherhood as the greatest profession, noting that "it incurs considerably fewer expenses than $70 per hour." And she reflected winsomely that there must be a lot of mothers out there who would be a lot happier and more conscience-free if they could only have a little more respect for homemaking as a profession and confidence in themselves as the best teachers of their own. The once-troubled mother is now a home-school leader in Indiana.

The One-to-One Advantage

Many parents readily surrender their "very bright" youngsters to the professionals. After school has been going for a time, some begin to wonder about sending their little ones off to schools which they often condemn—as if they themselves were condemned to so doing. There are, of course, good schools, a few of real excellence, but none of them can match the record of most good homes with warm, responsive parents who have teaching instincts. Few parents think that they do, and if the truth were known, most teachers fear that they don't.

The chances are that both parents and teachers who have such respect for this great profession are its best candidates. Yet you parents carry a great advantage because you work "one on one," while typical classroom teachers must deal with twenty, thirty, forty or more children under circumstances which oftentimes turn off learning more than they turn it on. Such teachers need our sympathy and encouragement more than the censure they so often receive.

Then there is the child. The curious, questioning one is usually the bright one. Yet, when he has to fit into a pre-molded educational program where he has to take his turn in class, there is bound to be some learning loss as compared to his being taught one-to-one in a warm, responsive home. Add to this all the extras required of most teachers, the total material they must cover, and the many different kinds of equipment they are under mandate to use, and there is little time left for person-to-person contact with their students.

In a 1983 study reported by Graduate Dean John Goodlad of the University of California at Los Angeles, it was found that the average teacher in 1,016 American classrooms responded personally to his students about seven minutes a day.[1] Elementary school children each receive from none to four or five responses per day, depending on how aggressive or assertive they are. In a reasonably loving and responsive home, the average family-schooled child often receives fifty to a hundred times as many adult-to-child responses.

No wonder, then, that such researchers and writers about genius as Harold McCurdy [2] either imply or declare again and again that the spring of brilliance and leadership flows mostly from the home. The classroom teacher who conducts his class along the lines of a good family—much like the old one-room school—and who uses the older to help the younger and the stronger to aid the weaker will generally be the most masterful and loved. Yet, in our blindness and thoughtlessness and worship of tradition, we somehow bring deep respect, even reverence, to school systems which were born in the home and today are dying in institutions. It is time that we retrace our steps to see where we have been and where we should be going.

The Fallacy of Assembly-Line Schooling

Most of us teach as we were taught; unfortunately, many of us were not taught well. So there are quite a few teachers who act as though teaching were a mechanical infusion of knowledge—as with a nipple, a teaspoon, a funnel, or a sledge. Many teachers thoughtlessly conclude that all children in the same class or of the same age should learn the same amount of the same things at about the same time and that they will come off the assembly line in about the same shapes with about the same equipment. It never occurs to them that some youngsters are "triangular," some are "cylindrical," some are "rectangular," and some are oddly shaped. But they try to drive them all through the same "square" hole.

Our children—in America, a trust "under God"—are caught in a system handed down by Greek and Roman philosophers which we randomly call the "liberal arts and sciences" or the "humanities," and which includes along with classics some occasional academic skills. Many glorify this traditional system. To them, a reading of the Harvard Classics makes a gentleman. The recent *Paideia Proposal* of *Encyclopaedia Britannica*'s Mortimer Adler largely espouses this theory of sameness and tradition.[3] It claims to be creative, but in fact turns off free exploration and proscribes genius at even earlier ages. Tradition has its place, but it must not be allowed to dampen creativity or to limit initiative in either child or adult.

For most youngsters (and even teachers), this Greco-Roman heritage is an exercise in endurance whose only meaning for them is that they will be accepted, conventional, and will be doing what everyone else is doing, with as much rivalry as can be developed in a system which cultivates more repetition than original thought. Expedience generally reigns. Principle—the basic reason for a conclusion—is ignored, because it is not known or even considered. It doesn't occur to many teachers that children should know *whys* and *hows.* Social pressure becomes the highest law, and in its train follow expedience, ignorance, and learning failure. This absence of thought and common sense in turn destroys creativity and brings a stupidity that breeds moral recklessness and decay.

The Ingredients of Great Teaching

Real teaching is loving. If you don't believe that love is the greatest teacher, read about Abigail Adams. She spent precious hours daily with her young John Quincy and saw that he had the privilege of work every day—that of running the mail to Boston during the American Revolution. When he returned, she sat down with him, side by side, to discuss events of the day, making the best of what books and manuscripts were available in his early years. Abigail loved young John Quincy into great learning. Her hundreds of daily responses were many more, perhaps hundreds more, than the best of classes provide today in institutional schools. And these responses meant the sheerest of educational power. Thus young J. Q. went to Harvard at age fourteen, without any institutional schooling.

Nor should this be considered so startlingly unusual today. In the fall of 1983, Grant Colfax left his rural Mendocino County home in northern California for Yale and, when he could not find the specific biology courses he wanted, he nursed his battered pickup truck to Harvard to study under full scholarship. Grant had never attended regular school during his elementary and secondary years. In fact, he has had no electricity in his home since he was five and did not start formal schooling at home until age eight. Yet, on the basis of his performance on the College Board Examinations, he was acceptable on full scholarship in nearly all of the Ivy League colleges and universities. His mother, Micki, notes that at home they gave him what books they could find, provided a heavy program of chores and many parental responses—which Grant shared with three brothers. All three of them (including one adopted black, and one Eskimo) are showing similar promise of genius.

Teaching is responding. A few years ago Dr. Marcelle Geber, a French scientist, went to Uganda where she examined youngsters in tribal communities and in upper-class homes.[4] Using Gesell tests from Yale University, she found that the little children who were close to their mothers and received constant warm responses scored significantly higher mentally, socially, and behaviorally than Western children. However, the upper-class children—generally cared for by nannies or placed in preschools, much as in the dictates of Western culture—were quite uniformly below the Western norms. The mothers' responsiveness is largely credited with making the difference.

In one of the most famous experiments on mental and social development, Professor Harold Skeels noticed that even though certain young orphanage children were given the most antiseptic care, they became more and more retarded, and some died.[5] He theorized that the sterility of the care may have been keeping them from the standard diseases, but it was not providing for their emotional needs. So he asked permission to place twelve little orphan girls in the care of retarded teenage girls (who were also in the custody of the orphanage). Each retarded teenager warmly took care of her particular charge as though the infant belonged to her. Although they were neither sophisticated nor certificated, they brought every one of the twelve infants out of her stupor to become healthy and attain an average or better mentality, later to marry and enjoy a normal family life. The orphans who did not have the benefit of this limited emotional response became more retarded and in some cases suffered an early death. Thus Dr. Skeels rightly concluded that the development of a child's mind depends far less on formal education than it does on warm responses.

Teaching is giving your child time to respond to you. Recent University of Florida studies verify that the best teachers wait longer for answers to their questions than do inferior teachers.[6] Effective teaching gives the student time to think. If a question is not worth the investment of a few extra seconds—or minutes or hours or days, in some cases—it is not worth asking. Many teachers allow only a split second, then give the answer themselves. Strong teachers allow at least four times as long. Each time you tell a child too much or do it *for* him when he can find out or do it himself, you stifle his creative potential.

Teaching is giving. Those who teach solely to earn a dollar, and not to provide kindness, to stimulate young minds, and to build children, should not wonder why today's literacy levels have been falling so consistently and fast since the nation started out on its program of learning pressures after the Russian Sputnik made its appearance in Western skies. Even the famed High/Scope studies at Ypsilanti, Michigan, which were supposed to bring credit to Head Start programs, actually found their best success by relating closely with the home and working in very small groups—with a skilled adult to every five or six children—rather than centering on typical Head Start store-front operations downtown. Concerned parents and teachers who understand that great teaching is warm responding and wise modeling, who become swept up in the beauty of the child's response, who teach in order to give more than take—are those who know the thrill of true teaching.

Teaching is understanding the needs of the ones to be taught. The University of Chicago's Benjamin Bloom did all kinds of factoring from a thousand or so studies that he reviewed. *At first* he decided that little children should best be hurried into school. But the professor either had not looked at his data carefully enough or had cradled it in biases. After the early-schooling movement had done irreparable damage by brainwashing parents into rushing their children out of the home into institutions, he had second thoughts. So he rechecked and expanded his research.

In 1980, to his immense credit, he came to the conclusion that the home is, in fact, the best educational nest, parents are generally the best teachers, and parents are educable.[7] Dr. Bloom had finally centered on the needs of children as they develop optimally in a beautiful symphony—mentally, physically, spiritually, emotionally, and socially. (See chapter 16, "How Children Develop.")

This does not mean to suggest that all homes provide these advantages, but rather that most of them can and more of them should. We must stretch our minds to understand what is happening and why! It is time for America's people, as world leaders, to place the home and the school in proper perspective. Greece failed to do this and decayed until it was destroyed. Rome followed Greece's tragic model, and later France fell into the same trap in the era of the French Revolution. If we do not undergird the home and set out deliberately to make it first in the lives of our children, *our* society, too, is in danger of dying. We can already smell the decay.

Teaching is exploring. Even more than books by themselves can do, teaching gives our children freedom to explore, much as little lambs out in the pasture. Teaching consists of providing many experiences in this pasture. Let your imagination go. Find a lesson in a teaspoon, a flower, a star, a grain of sand; in every personal experience—yours, your children's, your friends'. Note colors, odors, textures, sounds. Think of all the senses—taste, touch, smell, vision, hearing. All are involved in building a real live person. Teaching of this kind gives great breadth and depth; it offers the children "learning hooks" on which they can hang other learnings. And the more of these hooks they have, the more abundant will be their genius. *Most children who learn self-control and self-direction, guided by the responses of concerned parents, will have some obvious elements of genius.*

Teaching is being an example. This may be the most powerful teaching tool of all. Research clearly shows that young children who have the opportunity to learn from relatively few people, without the distraction of having many children about them, will be less confused and more certain of their direction. As pointed out by Dr. Urie Bronfenbrenner of Cornell University, the more individuals there are around the children, the less *meaningful* human contacts they will have.[8] Dr. McCurdy agrees, from his study of genius.[9] Children need the singular adult example which parents can best provide. If the parents cannot provide this, let the children—at least for the first ten or twelve years—have the relatively limited and selective influences of others, such as worthy grandparents or other trusted adults who have values similar to those of their family. (See chapter 19, "A Place for Grandparents, Too.")

Imparting formal academic skills and content, however important, is only a small part of teaching. For the first eight or twelve years, teaching should not be primarily from books. It is not simply learning how to add, subtract, multiply, or punctuate that makes productive citizens, crucial as these skills may be. It is not only learning the lessons of history and of how our government works, and of how many cubic centimeters there are in a cubic inch, and who won the Battle of Waterloo. It is also learning why most things fall instead of rise in the earth's atmosphere. And it is discovering that a hot stove may burn your hand, and that spending your savings on the first jalopy that is offered you may be a bad buy. It is learning that integrity is priceless, consistency is a jewel, and dependability is rarer these days than gold.

Teaching is using books discreetly. It is encouraging people to learn how to think. The person who teaches only *what, where,* and *when* may come to any kind of random conclusion. But when he asks *why* and *how*—when he asks for basic reasons—he is teaching *principle. Why* and *how* questions more often lead to deeper thought, and to understanding of principles, the basic reasons for our actions. Although this type of teaching seems to be rare these days, it is available to all, and most directly and successfully on the one-to-one basis that is afforded in the home. Books are important learning tools, but of all the methods listed in this chapter, they are the least powerful for the normal elementary—and secondary—school child who is still in basic

education. This may be hard to believe, but it has been true
for all of recorded history.

Character education is the missing link. The highest goal of
teaching at its best is character education. It is bringing to our
children/students lessons of love which breed concern for others—putting them ahead of ourselves. It is showing by example
that honesty, dependability, neatness, order, industry, and initiative pay richly. It is teaching the equality of human beings by
practicing the Golden Rule. It is demonstrating to children how
to work and how to help, instead of waiting for things to be
done for them. It is teaching them to feel needed and wanted
and depended upon—in order to develop a sense of self-worth.
The child who has this advantage generally becomes a self-
directed leader in his society. He knows where he is going and
is not easily pressured by his peers.

Debunking a Myth

It is not hard, then, to see that the greatest teaching is best
done "one on one." The best *remedial* teaching and the best
creative teaching have both been done this way for centuries.
The lives of John Wesley, Abraham Lincoln, Albert Einstein,
Agatha Christie, Douglas MacArthur, Pearl Buck, Hans Christian Andersen, artists Andrew Wyeth and his son, Jamie, are
examples of home-educated youngsters who were given the freedom to explore. They were not restrained in classrooms, which,
to many, are cages. They were given the freedom of the little
lambs or "kids" that they were. Their mothers and fathers lovingly shepherded them, warmly responded to them, and provided
sound parental examples. Thomas Edison, whose teachers considered him dumb, is a noted, if not notorious, example of a child
who found his mind and his body cramped by the classroom.
Fortunately, his mother accurately appraised his creative mind
and encouraged and responded to him at home.

The general impression that prevails today—that the best teaching is done in the classroom—is a devious myth, largely manufactured by people who are protecting their own jobs, by parents

who are rationalizing because they want to get their children out from underneath their feet, and by people who simply do not know better and actually think they are doing a public service. But now many mothers and fathers and professional educators are seeing this myth for what it is and are discovering that their responses, their example, and their supervision of free exploration are bringing out great children—academically, behaviorally, and socially. Any normal parent with a little curricular help can start his child on paths of brilliance which few classrooms can match. And, concurrently, the more that classroom teachers emulate a good home, the more successful they will be, regardless of their credentials and degrees.

Teaching is helping students learn to live and to become excited and motivated to learn more . . . and more . . . and more. Indeed, much excellent teaching is recorded by teachers in the classroom, but the best teaching of all—in proportion to the numbers of children involved in home or school and geniuses produced—is most naturally done by parents in the home, many of whom, probably like you, at first doubted their ability to teach.

3. How to Start Home Schooling, Whether or Not Your Child Is Already in School

FOR YEARS, a number of mothers in Grant County in eastern Oregon loaded their offspring onto yellow buses for caged rides that often lasted an hour or more. Then the state recently decided it could no longer afford such nonsense. It would pay for home-schooling curricula and let the parents teach at home. The main difference between these mothers and other beginners was that the state initiated their efforts. For most mothers there is a much stronger motivation—the conviction that they are doing the best for their children.

For generations, most states have been lenient about home schools. But as enrollments have dropped and teacher jobs are at stake, it has been more difficult for public and private school officials to let go of their subsidies, from either your taxes or your tuition fees. And the threat is more obvious when you withdraw your children from school than if you had never enrolled them.

In the past, most of our emphasis has been on parents' keeping their children at home, whenever possible, at least until age eight or ten or older. We have suggested ways to build a solid foundation for later formal schooling by a consistent, informal home program. However, as school problems and parental awareness of an alternative have increased, we have seen some spectacularly successful results of changing horses in midstream. So we have found that it is never too late to take children out of school (a) if you are committed to home schooling as a better alternative; (b) if you will be reasonably consistent, warm, responsive, and well organized in your program; (c) if you have a sound curriculum (see Appendix A of *Home-Spun Schools* for criteria); and (d) if it does not make them too unhappy to be separated from their friends. In almost every case, we have found that you can make your children content by providing such activities as trips with you while others are in school; involving them in family industries—making and selling things, or providing needed services—as officers in your family "corporation"; doing kind deeds for others; and fixing up a corner or room together for a "school." Other children will be quick to visit you. They know when parents care and children are happy. We suggest the following steps:

1. *Send a letter to the school,* timed to arrive on your child's first day of absence, explaining that you have decided to enroll your child in a private school. This is your *own* private school. It is a "school" because learning takes place, and it is as "private" as any available.

Generally speaking, keeping children home after a school vacation break is an opportune time for making the change. Such wise timing creates as little commotion as possible.

2. *Know your state law* and learn how to deal with local authorities in case it is necessary. You may eventually fulfill every letter of the law, if this is your desire, but you must first determine what that is from a sympathetic, knowledgeable source. Nearby home-schoolers may be your best source of information. (Hewitt Research Foundation can furnish lists of home-schoolers and support-group leaders, as well as information on state home-schooling policies. See Appendix A for further details.)

Because acceptance of home schooling varies so much among states, as well as in local districts, most experienced leaders advise against attempting to make any preliminary arrangements with school officials, unless you are very "visible" in your community and can't avoid it, and until you know about the local legal climate. We have found that even when statutory provisions are clear, superintendents may be prejudiced or may choose to ignore the law. At best, officials may try to dissuade you on the basis of your "inferior" ability and facilities, or your child's "need of socialization"—none of which is generally a valid reason. Most home-schooled children achieve significantly higher levels, academically, socially, and behaviorally, than public and church school students, and any possible disadvantages are nearly always far outweighed by the advantages. The U.S. Constitution, our basic law, supports you.

3. *Name your school.* Children like to share in this. Many names for home schools have special significance to the family and can give the child and parent a satisfactory answer to questioners.

4. *Use a "home-school curriculum,"* at least for the first year, especially if you have any doubts about teaching on your own. (See criteria and listing on pp. 144–45 of *Home-Spun Schools.*) This gives the structure to keep your program on a consistent track and a reasonable basis for equivalence to a regular school system, if you are questioned. However, on a one-to-one ratio, an hour and a half of parent-teacher time and about the same amount for supervised study is an adequate schedule for even the mature student. Afternoon is usually spent in constructive activities such as gardening, baking, homemaking, cottage industries, and so on, but should be listed on your program as practical arts, science, or other "subjects."

5. *Acquire previous school records.* This is actually optional, because you don't *have* to have the records, but it might avoid later problems. It also makes you the custodian of all pertinent documents. Your curriculum source will usually send for your child's cumulative records from the previous school, or you may ask for them yourself. Whether or not you use an outside school curriculum, you might want to have typed or printed official-looking school stationery. (Some home-schoolers use a post office box to make their location less obvious.)

6. *Write up your general philosophy, objectives, resources, methods, and schedule.* You will then be ready in case your "school" is challenged. Below is an outline used by one highly successful family which might be helpful as a guide in preparing a plan

of your own to have on hand in the event a school official should contact you:

I. **General Information.**
   A. *Children:* John Doe, Jr., born 1/6/72. Jenny Doe, born 4/9/74.
   B. *Name, address, and phone number of parents:* John, Sr., and Mary Doe, 654 Oak St., Dover, MS. Phone: 605-354-6090.
   C. *School(s) previously attended by children:* Dover Grammar School.
   D. *Attitude of the children:* John and Jenny understand the concept of home education and fully cooperate with the plan. Other friends and relatives are also taught at home, so they do not feel strange about it.

II. **Goals.**
   We want to prepare our children to be good citizens of our country, a credit to their home and to society. We feel that the best method for this is to educate the heart and the hand as well as the head, consistent with the requirements of God as stated in the Scriptures.

III. **Philosophy of Education.**
   We strongly believe that there are special benefits gained by the child from a quality home-education program, especially in his early years. For the state to deny the child this opportunity would deny him his basic rights and would be undue intrusion. The home school is the original school.

   We accept and practice the evidence published by the Hewitt Research Foundation of Washougal, Washington, and others based on sound research, common sense, and the high record of home schools in America (including George Washington, John Quincy Adams, Robert E. Lee, Franklin D. Roosevelt, Agatha Christie, General George Patton, and many others). This clearly indicates the wisdom of allowing flexibility in the program of a child under ten or twelve years of age to adjust to the child's readiness for formal education. In fact, some of those named above did not go to regular school at all until university age. Undue pressure to perform at a certain level before a child's vision, hearing, brain, nervous system, and social and emotional development are reasonably mature—and working together—often leads to learning disabilities. Risk is greater for boys, who generally mature a year or so later than girls.

For even more than academic considerations, we are concerned that our children develop firm Christian values before they are exposed to conflicting standards of behavior, as normally happens in a large-group situation. Until a child can reason consistently from cause to effect, he is very likely to copy the habits, manners, and speech of his peers. According to Cornell's Dr. Urie Bronfenbrenner, early exposure to this influence results in peer dependence, rather than in the child's developing a solid sense of self-worth, self-direction, and positive social values as part of the family corporation. And the child is vulnerable until at least grade six or age twelve.

Our children will not be kept in a social straitjacket. They will have proper association with neighborhood children and relatives, and will participate in church socials and other occasions which will provide ample opportunity to learn good social skills.

IV. **Resources.**

  A. *Qualifications of parents:* God has given us, as parents, the responsibility for ensuring the physical, mental, spiritual, and emotional health of our children so that they may become mature, productive members of society.[1] Our commitment to these principles and our love, example, and responsiveness to our children are our best qualifications.

  We gain our knowledge of child training from such Scripture verses as noted, and from careful reading of the following books on child development, among others: *Better Late Than Early, Dare to Discipline, Home-Grown*

Kids, and Home-Spun Schools. We have also attended a seminar on child training given in our church and closely follow the radio series on the family by Dr. James Dobson and by Tim and Beverly LaHaye.

In addition, Mary, the mother, has completed a high school education and has pursued a self-education process in fitting herself to be a teacher of her children. John, Sr., the father, has finished high school and technical school and helps in the teaching process with his skills in math and woodworking, inasmuch as his occupation is cabinet-making.

B. *Educational materials used:* Academic supplies are purchased from Hewitt-Moore Child Development Center, which individualizes a program according to the results of previous testing and a detailed questionnaire filled out by the parents. Teacher editions are also supplied, and sample work must be sent to the Center three times a year, to assure the director that adequate skills are being taught and mastered. The program includes the same subjects as normally studied in the public school—with the addition of the Bible.

We have also purchased supplemental educational aids, including a tape recorder and tapes of music, math instruction, and character-building stories. Our library consists of a set of encyclopedias, as well as numerous other books which are read by or to the children. We also have a variety of educational games on phonics, math, and spelling. For additional resources we use the local library, museums, manufacturing plants, and other places of historical and educational interest.

V. **Methods.**

We have much discussion of the material studied, emphasizing *whys* and *hows* to stimulate creative thought, instead of limiting instruction to *whats, whens,* and *wheres* (facts, dates, and places). We require more oral and written reporting than most regular schools can possibly have, but with less emphasis on workbooks. In other words, we are teaching our children to be thinkers as well as reflectors of others' thoughts.

We also have many field and nature experiences and we work daily together in a "cottage industry," teaching homemaking, minor repairs, and productive labor. We make and sell fruit cakes and leathercraft projects. This also makes our math lessons very practical. At least once or twice a week we visit the poor, old, ill, or infirm to build altruism into our children—giving them a practical understanding of the Golden Rule.

7. *Keep a daily journal of your activities.* Both you and your students should do this. It not only gives a good picture of organization to others, but also helps both teacher and child to be systematic and learn how to write. Besides, it can be fun now and provide fond recollections later.

So, be off and running, for you are on your way to the kind of education that kings use to make . . . kings!

4. Organizing and Stretching Your Time

NOT LONG AGO in our Portland, Oregon, seminar a mother of three asked in despair, "How on earth can I possibly do my housework and teach three little jumping jacks, too?" We called to the podium another mother, Mrs. Jeanine Ford. She explained simply how she did it with eleven of her own plus six foster children. She provided an excellent illustration of a mother who uses well-proven efficiency techniques. Before we outline them, we concede that Mrs. Ford had two important points in her favor: (1) she didn't stop to ponder whether or not she could do it, and (2) she had the enthusiastic support of her architect husband.

Modern mothers ask hard questions, as do some fathers. Society's pressure is heavy on them to make motherhood appear as drudgery, so naturally they need encouragement and sound answers. We think it is a very legitimate question to ask of us: "Okay, how can I blend housekeeping, home teaching and sound child rearing into a decent daily schedule, especially when I have very young children?"

Home-schooling families often enjoy living "next to the land." For both health and financial reasons, they do their own gardening, canning, and freezing of produce, as well as baking their own bread and preparing other foods from scratch. Add these nonautomatic activities to the usual laundry, shopping, cooking, and cleaning chores—not to mention visits from relatives and friends who schedule themselves into already "hopeless" days— and we concede that such home-schooling mothers are facing a mountain.

There are some who really find it impossible to cope with this kind of load and still hope to teach their own children. Sometimes, because of mismanagement, poor health, lack of organization, or sheer lethargy, these mothers are able to meet only the actual physical needs of their children. Time for reading or doing special projects with them seems out of the question. Yet, with study and commitment, most mothers can manage these duties with relative serenity and thoroughly enjoy the richness of spirit which far too few mothers these days care enough to know.

Father is important, too! It is usually the wife and mother who fills the home-teaching role, yet fathers are becoming increasingly involved. We know a single Michigan father of five who handles the home-schooling role magnificently. The children are well-fed, well-behaved, clean, and academically bright. During unemployment crises, many fathers have stepped in while the mothers worked. In any case, the family with a cooperative husband and father is more likely to enjoy a life that is a dream rather than a nightmare. We grant that home schooling requires work and dedication, but it does get easier as the children grow, especially when one learns how to train children from their earliest days to become assets rather than liabilities.

Here are some of the streamlined methods that have worked for others:

Scheduling

We have often heard mothers remark near the end of a summer, "I'll surely be glad when school starts, so life will not be so hectic." The opening of school forces the family into some kind of schedule in order to meet the demands of the school, and this automatically brings a certain stability to the home. We suspect that when school is not in session the home is more "freewheeling," which generally leads to frustration, confusion, and, sometimes, utter chaos. So why not keep your family on an even keel and find more peace and security for all concerned? "Schedule" is a bad word to some people. Perhaps school bells and other regimentation have created aversion toward the idea. The real question is whether we are willing to work in harmony with natural law or against it. The truth is that we can't toy with nature without paying a price. The universe in which we live is operated systematically and so are our bodies. Astronomers tell us that there has been no deviation in the orderly movement of the heavenly bodies in all of recorded history. Our bodies also run on a rhythmic cycle—sometimes referred to as circadian or daily body rhythm, or as the biological time clock.

We and our children function more efficiently when we are working closely with our body cycles. In order to make the most of our children's health, security, disposition, and discipline, it is vital that their meals and times for bed, naps, and baths be regular and consistent within reason. This is also basic for any smoothly run household.

Contrast such homes with families we know where the parents let the children stay up at night until they fall asleep and then let them sleep as long as they wish in the morning. Mother runs a fast-food service, since she feeds each one as he awakens—or whenever he asks for food—all day long. She can, of course, get little else done, and the effect on the children's health, and therefore their disposition and discipline, is devastating. Here are some reasons.

Mealtimes. As viewed under a microscope, the saliva in the mouth before a meal contains numerous enzymes and digestants.[1] After the meal, these elements are almost completely depleted, and it takes about three hours for them to be restored.[2] The cycle of bile production by the liver and for other digestants operates on much the same schedule. The entire digestive system needs a time for rest in order to function efficiently. Food in a normal meal, if consumed more often than about every five hours, is likely to be handled inefficiently by the stomach and therefore is subject to fermentation and other digestive disturbances.[3]

X-ray studies of the stomach show that normal emptying time of the stomach for a protein-vegetable meal is about four or five hours. Fruit and cereal without fat take less time. However, if the digestive process is interrupted by a snack before the stomach is emptied—no matter how high-quality it is—the stomach may have to work much longer before it becomes empty and can rest. Digestion is also hampered by drinking water or other liquids with meals, because they dilute the gastric juices. Drink plenty of water between meals and you will not be thirsty at mealtime.

Building the vital forces. Because irregular eating and sleeping upset the digestion, this in turn saps the brain forces and generally reduces efficiency—and learning potential. Regularity not only makes a brighter and happier child but also provides security because he knows what to expect.

Work out a reasonable schedule and stick to it the best you can. It may be hard at first, but keep trying. We have seen such changes solve a variety of family problems. It gets easier as time goes on, especially as you see your young ones catching on. Start by getting the children to bed early. Baths before bedtime seem to be standard in many families, and it is great when dad takes over here and follows through. This can be a close, happy time for him, especially when he has been gone or occupied with his business all day. Plan to have some stories, and—for the richest experience—have worship before final goodnights.

Taking Time to Plan

This evening respite will give mother time for planning meals and activities for the next day. Make a written plan on a bit of note paper. (At our home we keep 3″ × 5″ cards always available as organization helpers.) List tomorrow's events and menus in order, but don't be discouraged if things don't work out exactly as you anticipated. Teachers' lesson plans don't always either, so don't get too rigid or detailed. At least you are likely to accomplish the most important things, and leftovers can be listed again on a new paper for the following day. Some days will go better than others, but usually days that you plan will go more smoothly than days that "just happen."

If possible, you should plan a little time to do some things for yourself and with your spouse. Then get to bed early. This is just as essential for you as for your children, and will make it easier for you to get up early the next morning. In terms of personal efficiency, your morning time before breakfast is several times more productive for work and study than late evening time. Your body battery will much more strongly energize your mind. Religious families often prepare their spiritual batteries for the day by spending some time in study and prayer.

Up with the Birds

Get your children up early enough, if you can, to share a bit of morning time with dad before he goes off to work. If they are reluctant, play music or do something special to arouse them gently. They will gradually adjust. It is usually better if they get dressed before breakfast and have a very short worship time, appropriate to their ages. This can be done at the table before the "fast is broken." After a good breakfast—which should be the heartiest and most nutritious meal of the day—give them nothing except water until lunchtime.

Be sure to have the children help with the morning chores. Any normal child who can walk can help to do something, and it is important that he understands very early in life that he can contribute to the family team. This is an expected obligation about which there should be no question, but his help should be appreciated as a necessary and vital part of the family's well-being. Your children can help clear the table; rinse, stack, or wash the dishes; start the laundry; make beds; take out trash or garbage; vacuum and dust; and perform other basic housekeeping jobs. Take the time to teach the children carefully *how* to do this work. At first it will take you longer than if you did it yourself, since the children will not be as quick or efficient as you, but the time invested will pay big dividends, and soon you will find life much easier.

The morning chore time should have a predetermined limit, set by the clock, and should be about the same each morning, so that you can conduct school consistently—except, for example, when you have planned a field trip. All ages can participate in the opening exercises: Pledge of Allegiance to the flag, story, prayer, music, or whatever fits the lifestyle and beliefs of your family. If your children are age seven or younger, you may not have any formal schooling, but will involve one or more of them in a project you have planned such as gardening, baking, or other food preparation.

Teaching More Than One Child at a Time

If one or more of your children is eight or older, get them started on their school day with their book work, having them work as independently as they can. The younger children who are less involved with you as a teacher will need to be kept busy with coloring, painting, tools, or toys. Often one of the older children can play with or supervise the little ones while you teach the other older one(s). Be a teacher-manager and delegate responsibilities to your children, having them teach one another and alternating your attention between them as needed. Your younger children may enjoy listening in as you teach the others. This is great education.

The shepherd always knows where his lambs are, and is tender and kind. Yet every child should be trained from his first year to be happy doing things by himself. You do a disservice to your child if you let him feel that he must always be entertained or have someone's attention. We know of one mother who has an excellent solution when her boy says, "Mommy, I don't have anything to do. What can I do?" She answers, "Well, why don't you just sit right there and think for a while until you can figure out what to do?" She says he usually figures out something very quickly. Parents should not worry if their children occasionally seem bored. They may actually be reacting to some overstimulation which they have just had—television, too many visitors, or too much excitement. This may temporarily have dulled their creativity and ingenuity or caused them to become dissatisfied with simple pleasures. Don't be afraid to let them explore within the wise limits you set.

Skills such as reading, math, and spelling will probably need to be individually taught, but subjects such as the Bible, science, or social studies may be studied by all the children together, regardless of age. Activities, assignments, or projects in connection with these studies may be individualized according to ability, but all may learn about the same basic topic. (See chapter 11, "How, When, and Where for Your Child to Study Easiest and Best.")

Physical Education

Do you remember when children used to invent their own exercise games—climbing trees, fences and ladders; throwing balls to each other or over the shed or garage for "Ante-Over"; playing hopscotch, different kinds of tag, or informal just-for-fun races of hopping, skipping, four-legged, in burlap sacks, and so on? On their own, they made kites to fly, hoops or scooters to race, and stilts to walk or run on. Store toys, if any, consisted of little more than blocks, a ball, skates, a doll or stuffed toy, a wagon, a sled, and later a tricycle or bicycle. Most toys were for outdoor exercise. Urban life and ready-made toys have not only largely destroyed creativity but have left a vacuum for physical activity. Do whatever you can to provide adequate physical exercise for your children. Be careful about lessons in gymnastics or other physical skills which generally become too demanding and competitive. Park playgrounds, home equipment, and family activities and outings usually provide the best outlets.

A Time for Everything

As already mentioned, actual teaching time should probably take not more than an hour and a half daily, and total time for teaching and supervised study for older children need not exceed three hours (plus breaks). Voluntary reading, learning games, or construction-type projects can be done in other free time, as desired, but basics should generally be covered in the morning hours when the mind is ordinarily at its peak.

With help from any of the children who may not still be studying, prepare lunch at a regularly specified time. Everyone should help to clean up afterward, and then perhaps all could take part in a short walk or light exercise. Then it's nap or quiet time. As far as possible, each person should be alone and quiet, including mother, who should also have some rest. After a planned interval, she may spend a special time with one or more of those who are awake. Insofar as feasible, each child should have some undivided attention from each parent every day.

For the children who studied for most of the morning, there should be other constructive activities. These may include various home responsibilities, outdoor work, making things to sell, neighborhood jobs such as mowing lawns, shoveling snow or babysitting service. Work time should be about equal to study time. If dad or someone nearby has ability in woodworking, take advantage of the opportunity for children to learn this valuable skill; in fact, take advantage of any vocational skill which may be available for your child.

A Typical Home-School Day

The following, with variations, is a program followed by many families:

6:00	Arise and dress
6:45	Worship
7:00	Breakfast
7:45	Morning chores
9:00	Opening exercises for "school"
9:20	Reading
9:45	Math
10:15	Physical education
10:45	Handwriting/composition
11:15	Science
11:45	Social studies

12:15   Lunch
 1:30   Quiet time
 2:30   Practical arts and crafts, cottage industries, and/or free
        service time
 6:00   Supper (light and easily digested foods)
 7:00   Bath and worship or prayers
 8:00   Bed

Simplify Your Meals

Eat more natural foods—as nearly as possible the way they grow. Fancy desserts, casseroles, and other complicated recipes often take much of your time, yet are not necessarily the most healthful. Refined grains and sugar—found in white bread and sugared cereals—as well as free oils have had precious and irreplaceable ingredients removed. They rob the body of elements vital for optimum nutrition. For example, the outer 15 percent of the rice grain, which is normally removed in refining, contains 98 percent of the grain's vitamins and minerals which are necessary for good digestion and nutrition. Even so-called natural fruit juices are not as nourishing as the whole fruit and, in most cases, are more expensive than fresh fruit in proportion to the amount of nutrition obtained. Train children from infancy to enjoy wholegrain bread with little or no butter or margarine and cereals and fruit without sugar, and to avoid heavily salted food items.

Plan carefully for grocery needs so that you can do your shopping efficiently, preferably only once a week. Make a list, but keep it flexible enough to allow for special buys such as a seasonal choice of fresh vegetables or fruits. Avoid impulse buying and expensive snack-type foods with little or no nutritional value.

Streamline Housekeeping

Use as few dishes and utensils as practical. To save on dishwashing, use paper plates occasionally. You may even use paper napkins or towels as "plates" on which to serve a sandwich or other finger foods for simple lunches. If, for ecological reasons, you prefer not to use paper products, serve light meals on small plates which can be rinsed quickly and allowed to air-dry. Except for greasy foods, some serving plates do not require the total dishwashing cycle. Many folks who do not have an automatic dishwasher often wash dishes only once a day. This depends on your particular circumstances. Air-drying dishes in a drainer rather than towel-drying them saves time and is generally more sanitary.

Clutter is usually more of a housekeeping problem than is dirt. If you train your children properly, keeping it under control need not be a major task. Bookcases should be provided for books and toy shelves or boxes made available for toys. From the time they start to walk, children can be taught to put things away rather than leaving them all over the house. You, of course, will be the loser if you do not train them this way. Neither you nor they should feel comfortable with such disarray. It takes a little time at first, but it pays off, and is so much simpler to keep things in order—a place for everything and everything in its place.

Keep housekeeping chores to a minimum by removing dust-catching knickknacks, breakables, and any items requiring much care. Children can vacuum, dust, water plants, and even wash floors, if you show them how.

Personal Cleanliness

Some families wear out clothes more by washing them than they do by wearing them! Somewhere there is a happy medium between being downright dirty and unsanitary and being meticulous to the extreme. For instance, some particular families provide each child with a towel rack and a bath towel, hand towel, and washcloth of his very own. Each one is responsible for keeping his equipment neatly hung up and for washing carefully enough so that the dirt from his body or hands is not wiped on the towels. Every child receives a clean set weekly on a specified day. Other families allow children to use a clean towel for each bath. This usually ends up on the floor and in the laundry. Still other towels belong to everyone, and therefore must be washed more often. In the latter case, more laundry must be done, yet sanitation is much less satisfactory.

Underclothes and socks may well be changed every day, depending on the maturity of the child. However, with proper care, children's outer clothes need not be laundered as often as some mothers do. In some families, all the clothes a child is wearing go into the dirty clothes hamper each night, whether or not they are actually soiled. Bibs used at meals save washing by preventing food stains on clothing. When our children felt they were too old for bibs, we made them in a little different style, yet high enough under the chin to catch the spills, and we called them "aprons." Children can begin early to help with the laundry, as they learn to sort clothes, measure soap, and operate a washer and dryer, and then fold and put the clothes away.

Busy Hands Lighten the Load

Gardening and food processing not only foster health and economy but can be real fun. Very young children are seldom given an opportunity to be helpful in these projects. Get them started as young as possible, by carefully instructing and working with them. Let them plant and cultivate and weed, and watch their excitement! Let them harvest, wash, and snap green beans. Teach them how to tell the difference between the plants and weeds, explaining how the weeds choke out the good plants and take away the beneficial things from the soil. And tell them how the seed gives up itself so that it can multiply—and we can live.

In the kitchen, teach your children how to use a knife properly. When they are responsible enough, show them how to relate to your stove. Children of only seven or eight who have been given the right kind of experience and instruction can often bake bread or other foodstuffs, prepare entire meals, and even can or freeze produce by themselves. Never underestimate your children. We are constantly amazed at what young children are able to master in practical skills, but we also know that someone has spent a lot of time and effort in their training. You must be patient at first, for your child cannot possibly work as quickly and efficiently as you. Learn to accept his best job, though inferior to your own performance. You will find that, by age eight or ten, well-trained children can do most simple chores in a home, including meal preparation, care of their rooms, care of the yard, and minor household repairs.

If you really want to get organized, take time to sit down—first by yourself and then with your children—and plan things in the best order. For example, you could have the boys bring in the wood and then you will cut their hair, *before* someone cleans the kitchen floor. Make your list. Then work your plan. And change your names from Mr. and Mrs. Fumblebuss to Mr. and Mrs. Efficiency.

5. How to Go About Teaching at Home

ONE OF OUR New York home-schooling mothers said she had an inferiority complex about her teaching. It was really about her "education." She was normally a confident, articulate woman, but she had been thoroughly brainwashed by society's warning that only a college-trained, certificated person is competent to teach children. And she was "a mere high school graduate." The doubts of her neighbors finally got to her, so she hired a professional to take her place in her home school. Within a few weeks, irritations were popping up all over. This mother simply blamed herself and somehow scraped through the year—with a very ordinary scholastic record and children who were fit to be tied. "That year taught me," she wrote, "that the teacher was not doing anything I couldn't, so I took over. We had a great time in school."

You, too, are capable of teaching your child at home if you are willing, concerned, and systematic. Yet if you feel a little less than confident, you probably should enroll your child or children in a good curriculum at least for the first year. Check the criteria in Appendix A of *Home-Spun Schools.* It includes the requirements of a custom-made course of study for each child. However, a good program is more a system of teaching than a set of books, and this is what we want to help you understand.

Using Books Creatively

The study of books is *only a part* of your child's education—and in some respects the least part. Life experiences are usually far more important. These experiences, initiated by both children and parents and involving specific activities and general exploration, are the flesh and blood of true education. We suggest that you look at books with these ideas in mind:

1. *Make books your servants.* In no case should you and your child become their slaves. And minimize workbooks! Too many will stifle creative thought.

2. *Don't necessarily use the entire book.* Sometimes you will begin at the front of a book and work through it. In some instances, only *parts* of a book need be used—and not necessarily in order. In math, for instance, *Math-It* should have priority if you want to develop real skill. When Vicky Locke told our seminar what *Math-It* did for her boy who was having trouble with math, all our copies sold out in a few minutes. Don't hesitate to apply the information in the book to your practical needs. For example, on the day you plant your garden or lay your new rug, you may choose a part (perhaps even in the back of the book), dealing with calculating the size of areas.

3. *Combine learning from real life with source books,* to discover additional and unusual facts and to build genius.

Making a Schedule

Parents who have consistently maintained an organized household will find little problem in bringing classwork into the daily schedule. If you think of the book work as part of your housework—an extension of your daily routine—much of your stress will be relieved when you first attempt to set up your schedule. Remember, when you start your formal program, you need only an hour or two daily, including breaks, for face-to-face or side-by-side teaching. This might be in intervals of fifteen or twenty minutes at a time, rather than at one stretch. Include supervised study (teacher on call) for another hour and a half. A "beginner" would probably spend most of his time with you, of course, and not study this long until he gains more physical maturity and some independence in his work.

Assuming that you are a loving and responsive parent, this is very high quality time for your child, with much more attention than he would receive all day from a teacher in the classroom. Home-taught children on a daily program, as suggested in chapter 4, usually achieve much more than schooled youngsters.

Getting Organized

Probably nothing else is more essential for a good learning environment than the organizational structure of the total home. The home *is* school, and school is part of *life*. When your child awakens, goes to sleep, helps with chores, practices an instrument, or works in the garden, he is engaging in the most important schooling for living. You teach him the relative importance (or unimportance) of a clean home, for instance, by whether or not he usually picks up his clothes or tidies up the kitchen before he opens his books. Your school is best begun with the house in order. Sweeping the floors in an efficient way, making the beds without lumps under the covers, putting away the leftovers from a meal—all are part of crucial "home economics" for life and deserve high priority in the daily routine.

From observing your own devotions (the earlier in the day the better) your child will have "caught" rather than been "taught" the value of personal meditation or worship, and he will want to take part once he is old enough to read and pray on his own. Establishing an Absolute Source in whom to trust is the foundation on which all learning should start. It will help bring full meaning to American history when he can know by personal experience the trust in God on which our country was founded.

Whether or not your family is religious, we encourage you to lead your children in acting out character-building stories— secular and religious—or musical selections. Many character-story cassette tapes are available for their thoughtful learning.[1]

Children who begin while young are more likely to maintain this habit pattern consistently throughout life. Prayer and verse—whatever your religion, whatever way you choose—can also set the tone for the opening exercises of school along with the Pledge of Allegiance and national anthem, whatever your country. Other studies will then follow in reasonable order.

Although you should have a schedule prominently displayed in your "classroom"—one very much like the traditional school schedule—you will not be limited in carrying it out in a way that is necessary in a classroom of twenty-five or thirty students. At Hewitt Research Foundation, we are more interested in the total structure and response pattern of your home than in having a strict, unvarying school schedule. We would much rather know that you are giving ample time to work activities, that your meals are regular, that your child goes to bed on time and gets up early enough in the morning to have a good breakfast, comb his hair and help you with the morning chores before school, than we are in knowing that you start school exactly at 9:00 A.M., that you had recess precisely at 10:30, or that you had math on the dot at 11:00.

Within the structure of the school time, you can be rather flexible, yet consistent in the subjects where there is weakness, not letting slide any subject area in which review and drills are necessary for progress. For example, beginners should probably read every day. Consistent review is vital for learning.

Teaching through Chores

As with books, so with schedules: Be sure that they are your servants, not your masters. When boxes of pears are turning a golden yellow on the back porch, or a neighbor calls with the news that you may have all the green beans left in his garden, or the local farmers need help picking berries, your school day will take a very practical turn while you and your students become harvesters. Never feel that you are delaying school, for you are only enriching it with the highest type of teaching—working with your child. In the process you will profit by spending a few moments determining what lessons you would like to have your children learn about harvesting, preparing and preserving food.

One fall, a mother was motivated to teach her daughter at home primarily so that she could help her on a one-to-one basis to earn a scouting badge in the preservation of food. If your children are already reading and writing at such a time, have them write a letter to Grandma or other relative or friend, telling about the good things they were able to can that day.

Don't forget your journal or diary! It will be fun to read a few months or years or generations later. Have your children tell how many quarts they canned, froze, gave away, or prepared for dad's favorite dishes. For an arithmetic experience, have your children convert the number of pints of green beans into quarts, and so on.

The very quality of the work you do *with* your child is related to how much you actually work with him. If you peel pears with him, or direct his packing of fruit into jars while you scald the lids, the learning will be much more productive than if you put the child to work pitting cherries in the back yard while you run the show in the kitchen.

Several things can be done to make practical work a real learning adventure. First, as much as possible, progress from the work to books, rather than from books to work. However, after the child reads about something in a book, then encourage him to go on to apply the information he has found. When questions arise as the child does a job, be prepared with encyclopedias and other resource books where the *why*-and-*how* answers can be found. Use your town library if your own is scant. Answers can be shared with the family at the dinner table, in letters to pen pals or family members away from home and, of course, in his journal or diary.

Second, whatever your religion, pray daily for alertness to talk with your child as you work together. This is a good time to ask the child questions, to show interest in his feelings and problems. While the hands are busy and the mind is somewhat free, you will often find that your child will reveal inner thoughts that would never be shared over a desk or while seated in the living room.

It may be appropriate for you and your child to learn a great quotation or a poem or Bible verse while working. Garden work can often lead into spiritual truths and lessons. For example, hoeing together along the rows of emerging green plants might provide the opportunity to teach patience and endurance by your encouraging example. Also remember that children handle big jobs that have been divided into bite-sized pieces better than large total tasks—which sometimes overwhelm even an adult. Just the presence of someone working alongside is often enough to spur children to persevere to the end. Help your child feel the thrill of finishing a job and doing it well.

Keeping Careful Records

Obtain any former records your child may have accumulated and continue to keep scores of the tests you administer. Also keep health records. It would be wise to maintain a portfolio containing samples of your child's handwriting, creative writing, and other completed work, including a record of field trips (to a store, the fire department, the park, the zoo, and so on).

Your own records should be kept in a simple log book or journal listing dates and one or more significant activities or events about each school day. This might include a particular breakthrough in terms of a child's learning, a new concept introduced or an old one mastered, some very special work, field trip, or project.

Order in Learning

We mature and learn in a natural sequence. For example, *receptive language is learned before expressive language.* We all know that babies understand a lot of concepts long before they can verbalize those things. Thus, if we want to lower the level of difficulty, it is important that we ask children to choose between two alternatives, rather than asking them to come up with a particular word to answer a question or pick out a right answer from a group of answers, as in a multiple-choice question.

Another rule in the order of learning is that oral material is easier to do than written. Little children can tell lots of stories before they can write them. Sometimes in our desire to hurry the process we unwisely expect them to write down everything that they can say. Start in small steps. For example, first have them look at a picture and then tell what they are seeing in it. Have them tell you or the whole family or their neighborhood playmates something important that they are able to verbalize. Then have them write one sentence that tells something significant. Later on, ask for two or three sentences. If a child says, "I don't know what to write," have him *tell* you what he would like to say. Stop him at the end of the first sentence, and have him put it down. If you have the equipment, have him tape his sentence and listen to it several times. Then turn the tape recorder off, and have him write it down. Little by little the children will become young authors.

Laws of Learning

Remember the old saying "You can lead a horse to water, but you can't make him drink"? The perfect parallel is: "You can send a boy to school, but you can't make him think." Some things cannot be forced, and learning is one of them. Positive academic learning takes place only when the individual is ready, receptive, and cooperative.

There are some fundamental laws of learning that you can apply to make you a more effective teacher. Make them a vital part of your daily program:

1. *Children learn through their senses*—hearing, vision, touch, taste and smell. These channels can be sharpened by the proper stimulation but dulled by too much or too little. For example, ears trained to hear bird songs will recognize a particular call even in the midst of city noise. Or when one has studied trees, the eyes are quick to notice the variety of foliage, color, shape and beauty which untrained eyes fail to appreciate.

2. *Children learn best by physical, hands-on experimentation.* *Active* learning is needed to discover and solidify knowledge. It is said that we remember 10 percent of what we hear, 50 percent of what we see, 75 percent of what we say, and 90 percent of

what we do. This is true of everyone, but particularly of young children who actually need physical, hands-on experimentation. Passive learning such as educational television seldom produces creative scholars.

3. *Children learn by imitation.* They adopt the personality, attitudes, manners, habits, language and even the tone of voice of those persons who are dominant in their lives. In addition, until their values are stabilized and they are able to make reasonably independent decisions about acceptable or unacceptable behavior, they need to be protected from negative influences and exposed to consistent, sound parental models who exemplify worthy values and seek to develop them in their children.

4. *Children learn by repetition.* Simply introducing a concept does not constitute learning. If taught recently, it may be remembered, but then be totally forgotten if not soon repeated or reviewed. The greatest loss occurs after the first exposure, so the next review should follow reasonably soon—even as soon as the end of the class period, depending on the concept or process involved. Review must be continued until mastery is obtained, and then occasional review is necessary for permanency.

5. *Children learn to live up to the expectations of their parents and other adults.* They possess a built-in desire for approval and with reasonable motivation will attempt to achieve your goals for them. Handling this properly takes much wisdom. If your level of expectations is too high and your child feels he can never gain your approbation, he may give up. On the other hand, if your goals are too low, they will not challenge him to do his best. Law #6 is the next logical step.

6. *Children learn best when they are successful.* Whether the project is in academic learning, physical work, or character development, the child needs to feel that he is making progress. Verbal rather than material rewards are most desirable, and the accomplishment rather than the child should be commended. Everyone enjoys having his work appreciated.

7. *Children learn best when they feel secure.* This is best provided by consistent parenting in a warm, responsive home with a systematic program. For a child, routine is like the skeleton which supports the body; it is framework to depend on.

8. *Children learn what they can understand.* Difficult concepts are forgotten quickly or ignored. Young children learn first about home, family, and nature. These concepts, which become familiar to them in their early years by active exploration and experiences, form the learning hooks on which they can hang other information. When this background of practical, hands-on activity is sparse or nonexistent and language development is scant, we say that the child is deprived. Programs such as Head Start have been organized to compensate for such neglect. However, only if the home is highly involved do these methods produce any lasting academic recovery.

9. *Children learn what is interesting to them.* Parents often notice that children who do not seem to have a long attention span in some things can hardly be pulled away from others. The key is to start the learning where the interest lies or devise ways to make the subject interesting.

10. *What children learn must be used in order to be retained.* As soon as possible, put into practice what has been taught, either by doing something with the knowledge or allowing your child to teach it to another. Many parents have achieved mastery or discovered new understanding of a subject by teaching it to their child and a child can experience the same happy result. (See chapter 6 on cross-age teaching.)

Do plan some opportunities for oral expression. Once or twice a month, schedule a special time for your children to put on a little program for grandparents, the people next door, elderly people in a nursing home, or whomever is available. Let the children recite a poem or act out a Bible story they have been studying, plan a special worship time for the family or present a program which tells about some faraway place they are studying. The audience needn't be large—just enough people so that the children feel that someone is listening, and they are challenged to do their very best.

The Unit Method

Science, social studies, religion or any topic consisting of "subject matter" can be studied by using a single textbook and moving through it with the aid of a workbook to record the facts your child gleans from the reading. This is the traditional way. However, the unit method of organizing the day's learning activities around a single topic is considered to be one of the most effective methods of teaching. It is extremely practical for your child for finding any information he may ever need. It is particularly useful when you are teaching several children of varied ages. Even preschool youngsters can be included in the informal part of such a method. The unfolding of the procedure should follow as much as possible the creative approach of the children rather than be overly dominated by the adult.

A unit of study may be as simple as preparing a meal (including menu planning, marketing, cooking, serving, and cleaning) or as complex as the study of your state (including its history, geography, government, and economics). The choice of a topic may be triggered by a story or textbook chapter that invites further exploration, by an experience, or merely by natural curiosity or need.

Along with you, their teacher, the children should choose the subject they wish to study, establish their purpose in choosing it, plan activities or experiences which would be appropriate for the subject, and think through the kinds of materials or equipment needed and how to acquire them. If the unit of study requires maps, pamphlets, and other informational material which must be sent for, this may be one of the first activities to accomplish. Rather than confining the study to one book, information may be accumulated by reading in parts of several publications—encyclopedias, newspapers, magazines, and library books—finding pictures, exhibits, film strips, tapes, or other visual aids which provide information; interviewing or writing to knowledgeable people; or taking field trips.

Every unit should contain as many as possible of the following activities in balance: reading for skills, information, and enjoyment; observing; experimenting; listening; writing; oral expression through reporting and storytelling; problem-solving; making and using visual aids by preparing illustrated notebooks, maps, models, charts, or graphs; arts and crafts; music; poetry reading;

discussion, evaluation and sharing of learning; construction work employing fine and/or large-muscle groups; and presentation of the learning to someone outside of the school group. The unit should include the skills of penmanship, spelling, punctuation, capitalization, grammar, and even math and art.

A unit of study could be planned to last a few days, a week, a month, or longer, but ideally should be evaluated often and culminated by a proper conclusion—an activity of sharing, a summation of what has been learned, or the completion of a construction project. Though such a method may overflow into many different learning areas, it may not necessarily eliminate other routine studies that constitute the basics. It simply helps the child understand how very essential these skills are in finding and using information that one needs in order to become knowledgeable and practical in today's world.

Key to Success

We wish we might give you one key to ensure the success of your school. The great majority of home-schoolers are religiously oriented, so they feel the presence of a personal Divine Power. We agree and also find these home-schoolers easiest to defend in court. These parents are astonishingly successful, but those who are not "religious" also do amazingly well. The home school, properly conducted, is a remarkable tool for all.

At the end of your first school year, you will find that you will have learned perhaps as much as your children. Your students will be your best teachers, so listen to what they say and learn from your errors. Don't let mistakes discourage you. You're going to become a much better person because of your experience. It won't be easy, but it will be a challenging road with surprising turns and a reward at the end. And you will know that you have had a very important part to play in the character development of the little ones in your trust.

II. Some Teaching Secrets Not Commonly Practiced

6. Using Older or Stronger Students to Teach the Younger or Weaker

IN 1968, AT THE University of Chicago, some of us were invited to a "premier showing of a creative film on an intriguing new development in education." Actually the idea was millenniums old. It was cross-age teaching. This student-to-student teaching continues to be one of education's finest tools and one of its greatest economies. The wonder is that it is not more fully valued and more often used in both home and institutional schools.

The best teaching situation for basic education usually derives from a smaller student-to-teacher ratio than exists in most traditional programs. Normally this means hiring more teachers and higher expenses, so it has been more a frustration than a hope except for expensive private schools. But this is not so with home-schooling, which naturally provides the smallest of ratios and is usually better than the best of institutions. Large families often use the older child to teach the younger and the stronger to help the weaker. Moreover, the classroom of the average school can also more nearly approach the one-to-one advantage of the home school by such cross-age teaching.

This advantage holds true throughout the range from pre-schooler to college student. Would you like to teach your four-year-old to tie his shoes? Your six-year-old can probably do a faster and more trouble-free job than you. A standard requirement in our university classes was to require our child-development students to teach a three- or four-year-old an exercise in coordination and manipulation. Horace Tuttle, one of our mature graduate students known widely for his ways with children, reported to the class his deep frustrations and chagrin. He had chosen the apparently simple exercise of teaching his three-year-old son how to swing. After several days he had failed to teach his child how to "pump" in a swing. It required the skill of reverse coordination. In the midst of his frustration, Horace's five-year-old showed up with a cheerful "Let me show him, Daddy." In a few minutes the three-year-old was merrily swinging by himself.

For one thing, children are often less threatened by other children than by adults—especially teachers. Size, age similarity, recency of learning the skills themselves, and a general understanding of child by child seem to account for this phenomenon. And the child teachers don't even have to be bright. Dr. Harold Skeels, as previously noted, while experimenting with retarded but warmhearted teenagers, found that they brought declining toddlers back to strong and balanced development and sent them on to live normal, fulfilled lives—whereas the other toddlers who were left in the sterile care of adult professionals wasted away. The difference was more in the quality of responsiveness than in mental or academic competence. (See also chapter 2, "How You Develop Confidence as a Great Teacher.")

It has been proven in practice that a student can often induce learning in a fellow student more effectively than can an adult teacher. This may be done in a variety of ways and at virtually all school levels. The master teacher, then, becomes more of a teacher-manager who delegates teaching duties and supervises the work of many "teachers." This is true cooperation—the joint operation by teacher and student. It leads to self-respect and the desire to excel and avoids many pitfalls through building a sense of responsibility in all concerned.

This is a common practice around the world. The Soviets have long used teenagers to help younger students, and American colleges have for generations practiced cross-age teaching at all levels. In the elementary schools, peers are at least as powerful as adults (if not more powerful) in their ability to influence the behavior of our children.

This method may not be altogether effective in some subjects, but it is hard to imagine one. It can bring superior results in most standard elementary, secondary, and college studies. Students do not necessarily have to be older than the ones they teach, but they are usually stronger in the subject matter.

In this program of teaching by students (preferably in a nongraded situation if the school is at the elementary level), the teacher organizes the students into the teaching program as needed. He or she makes careful judgments of the students' performance, and at any point in the year may determine that a student has satisfied reasonable standards in a given subject. The teacher continually assesses the performance of his or her students, organizes them to assist in the teaching, and enriches their studies by giving them wider opportunities to explore. The following is an example at the high school level:

John has an excellent background in mathematics, radio, electronics, and so on, but is poor in English. He soaks up the standard physics work in one or two months, and his teacher uses him to tutor in physics during and after school.

Carl, on the other hand, has a fine home (and school) background in English grammar and is a talented writer. But he seems hopeless in physics and math. Since his teacher is taking advantage of every student's need for success, Carl is asked to teach English to John. But Carl is also John's student in both mathematics and physics. Since Carl performs above the other students in communications skills, he is not required to take any further high school grammar or composition courses. Rather, he uses his time (a) to enrich his already proven talents, (b) to catch up in areas where he is slow, and (c) to help teach other students in his areas of competence. He may continue this type of program from the elementary grades through high school and college.

In any event, *individual attention,* even by other children, is by far the greatest basic method for the development of strong students, including future scientists, scholars, and political leaders. The large school will seldom even closely approach the small one in this respect. The tutorial system, even with a child in charge, has never found its equal in teaching excellence.

7. Making the Teaching of Reading Easy

A YEAR AFTER Dorothy Moore was hired as a primary grade teacher at California's South Whittier schools, a routine school-wide achievement test alerted the principal to her unusual ability in the teaching of reading. He asked if she would like to be the school's reading specialist. She was delighted and before long was knee-deep in "problem kids." Most of them were little boys—who generally trail little girls in maturity and come up with learning failure and delinquency at least three or four times as often as girls. Soon Dorothy's success changed from "unusual" to "phenomenal," and eventually she was conducting seminars around the world. Research was added to this clinical experience, as she searched for simple answers to complicated problems. Soon she found that children who are allowed to mature until at least eight to ten do not really need much formal teaching of basic reading, and almost any reasonably sound method will work. Many younger children will actually learn to read without any instruction at all—if you will consistently read to them from a very early age.

When we find a child who is failing in reading, we know that we have one who (a) was immature in his reading tools when he was started into formal reading, (b) is hearing or vision impaired, (c) has been pressured, (d) is afraid and feels defeated, (e) needs new hope and confidence, and/or (f) first needs remotivation and restructuring of his perceptions, rather than simply a larger dose of the same thing he has been failing in. So we ask Dorothy Moore to tell you here how to meet these needs for both normal and reading-failed children:

ANY PARENT WHO CAN READ CAN TEACH READING

The ability to read is basic to almost all other learning, but we are finding a high rate of illiteracy in our nation. Children graduate from high school without adequate skills, so remedial classes in reading and writing are needed in college. Children are being labeled "dyslexic" or "learning disabled"—terms we hardly ever heard about a number of years ago. There seems to be no real explanation for this, although many are getting panicky about it. "Dyslexia" has been stretched to become a convenient label for "learning disability," much of which *we* cause by rushing our little ones into school too early, or by otherwise pressuring them.

The schools have tried all kinds of innovative methods—ITA, SRA, no phonics, all phonics—and we have sent children to school earlier and earlier and started the same academics in kindergarten as we used to teach in first grade—which was already too early. We are now getting more and more nursery schools and Head Start programs that are academically oriented. But the results are worse, not better. And what are the educators thinking now? "If we can just get them still earlier," they cry. Current recommendations of the teacher unions to cure our educational mediocrity includes starting school at age 3 or age 4 and lengthening both the school day and the school year. In fact, in Missouri the governor's task force was urged to have the professionals take charge of the children at birth. Under this plan parents could have custody as long as they follow the dictates of the State.

Why shouldn't these innovations work? If you are turning manufactured goods, a better tool or a better procedure on the assembly line often does improve the product, get it out more efficiently or reduce the cost. But when we are dealing with little children, we need to think more like the farmer plans. When the farmer plants his garden or his field, he thinks about what seeds, plants and insects are going to do anyway. He knows that he will get best results by adapting to their peculiar needs and characteristics. Thus with children. If we know that certain laws govern their development then it would be wise to obey them.

Research also says so. We have analyzed over 8,000 early childhood studies, in addition to our basic research at Stanford and the University of Colorado Medical School.[1] So we reason: if this research is correct, why aren't we following it in our educational systems? The truth is that in the field of education we have a wide gap between research and practice. If this were true in the business world of pharmaceutical houses and auto makers, the courts would be filled with charges of criminal negligence. Yet, in education, we pay relatively little attention to research. We respond instead to political, economic, and social pressures. For example, the trend toward earlier schooling seems designed to get more mothers into the work force and to provide teacher jobs at the expense of the children.

Two principles which child development research clearly supports are *first,* that the success a child will achieve in learning any particular skill is dependent upon his maturity—his mental, physical, and emotional readiness; and *second,* that the child becomes competent in a much shorter time when he is older than when he is younger. Many of you have watched these principles operate in your own families. You can work very hard to teach a child a certain skill at an early age, such as crawling up the stairs. But if you just wait a while he will learn it largely by himself. This principle operates in the development of coordination, reason, math, and even reading. It seems evident that we should try to discover more about what children really need instead of imposing adult standards on them; then move ahead to assist by being good examples and responders. In other words, read *to* them and *with* them.

Dr. Joseph Wepman of the University of Chicago says that America could reduce reading failure to 2 percent if we were to delay formal schooling until at least age eight or nine—much like Norway.[2] Yet we know from University of Texas studies that more than 20 percent of U.S. adults are functionally illiterate, and another 30 percent are doubtful.[3]

The actual reading method is not so important as the readiness of the child. This seldom if ever occurs before the senses and various functions of the body become mature and reasonably integrated around the ages of eight, nine or ten. We call this the "IML"—the Integrated Maturity Level.[4] When the child has achieved this (and it is pretty easy to tell by his response to your reading to him and by his questions), most any sound method will work. The most successful reading teachers use a combination of methods—an eclectic approach.

Read to Your Child

Of course, early experiences of a child's life do make a big difference in his ultimate success in reading. First, read to your child from as early as five or six months. The Michigan Reading Association has a bumper sticker that says, "Children who read were read to."

A very simple picture book is a good place to start. And you will likely get your best attention at this point by singing the text, making up or adapting some tune you already know or singing a song which fits the picture. In an incidental manner, you will help him see that you read from left to right—possibly moving your finger under the line and across the page as you read. Remember that there is nothing built into the human brain that programs one to do this. Japanese printing moves from top to bottom and right to left.

Later he will ask you questions, especially if you read the books he wants you to read. And what does he want you to read? The same one or two books over and over again. You read them until you are weary of them, but if you leave out a page or a line to get it over with sooner, he will remind you. Pretty soon you just give the book to him and let him read it to you. Or he will start asking questions, "What does this say,

Mommy?" or "Is this the line that says so and so?" or "Look, this word is the same as that one." He just starts figuring out some of his own little methods. You don't really know just how he does it, but he learns to read.

We call this the "natural" method, a phenomenon usually occurring in a warm, responsive reading-and-learning environment, but without "teaching" as such. Why not? How do children learn to speak? Do you teach them in any formal way? No, you just talk to them, and they learn to speak by being spoken to.

Be a Good Example

We also know that parents who show an interest in books and have many books around do make a difference. Developing a love for reading and finding out that books are important are things a child learns by example. For instance, suppose your child asks you a question whose answer you really don't know. Most of a child's questions can be answered right off the top of your head, but it might be well sometimes to say, "Well, let's see what the encyclopedia (or the dictionary) says." This is one of the most important things for everyone to learn—how to find needed information.

Provide Experiences

Most parents feel they have bright children. It is so easy for them to think that because they are bright they ought to go to school. Children may indeed be high in intelligence, but they are lacking in experience. Even bright children need to be working with you and having a variety of experiences, in order to build an interest in and an understanding of what they will eventually read.

Build Vocabulary

Do you know why Head Start children are considered deprived? They don't have this foundation of experience and language development. Many parents of such children don't even talk to their little babies because they figure they don't understand anyway. There may also be some who do not have good physical care, but even if parents do keep them clean and well fed, many do not respond or involve their children in the everyday experiences of the household and community. However, because the influence of the home is so basic and so all-pervasive, Head Start has difficulty in compensating for omissions which started at birth. The obvious solution for this is parent education.

At one time the government operated "Home Start," where the paraprofessionals—not professionals, but trained lay persons who were adaptable to this—would go into homes with toys and books and work with children and parents. They would teach the mother, for example, to read to the child expressively and responsively (because *how* you read to the child is important). They would also show them the best use for some of the educational toys. Sometimes they would show the mother how to use homemade items to teach the child.

After a two-year program, they held a closing convention of this experiment, which we attended. It was shown that Home Start was much more cost-effective than Head Start.[5] Positive effects were noted not only for the target child but also for the other children in the family. It was also good for the mother, helping her to have a better self-concept. Its influence spread throughout the community, bringing noticeable improvement. Yet this early version of Home Start did not survive, according to some evaluators, because it was not as politically expedient as Head Start.

Talk and Let Him Talk

Language development is another basic prerequisite for reading, and it starts at birth. Most mothers talk naturally to their babies and encourage them when they begin to coo and make sounds. These beginnings of speech make a lot of difference in the child's preparation for reading. You are his model, since he will copy your pronunciation, enunciation, and manner of speaking. He should be given much opportunity for expressing himself as he grows older—to tell events in sequence and organize his thoughts. Help him build a vocabulary—mainly by example, but also in describing and explaining current items of interest.

Recently our two-year-old grandchild closed the drapes in his room at naptime. I said, "Oh, that makes it dark." When he opened it up, I said, "Oh, that's good; it's light." The next day at naptime, when he pulled the drapes, he told his mother "dark" and when he opened them up he said "light." That was just one easy lesson in learning opposites. By experiences, children need to understand similarities and opposites, such as "above/below," "tall/short," "over/under," "high/low," and so on.

Develop Listening Skills

Another important preparation for reading is to teach your child to listen. Listening is a skill which is just as subject to improvement as any other skill, and it may be improved at any age. Most of us are really not very good listeners, but few of us realize this fully. And therein lies the cause of many arguments and misunderstandings. If you are a normal person or family member, you have some communication problems when you say, "I'm sure I told you that," or "I didn't hear you tell me that," or "That isn't what you said!"—because sometimes when we are preoccupied we don't even hear what the other one says or at least it doesn't make any kind of an impression. And other times we say one thing, thinking we said another.

Teach your children to listen actively and to associate what they hear with what they already know. Active listening is important for retention. For instance, you know you usually get more out of listening to a lecture by making some kind of notes on it than you do when you just listen. Similarly, little children should be encouraged to report on what they have heard, asked to repeat instructions they have just been given, and even retell some of the stories that they have heard. Remember, good listening habits are a key to efficient learning, whether learning to read as a beginner or listening on the adult level.

Enunciate Clearly

If you want your children to speak well, it is crucial for you to sound your words clearly. Be careful to use full lip movements and to be alert and consistent in catching your children's responses. Exaggerate your lip action. Make it a habit, like the best of broadcasters and actors and speakers.

In our own experiences of growing up, this was the way of life, even though neither Raymond's parents, nor mine, had extensive education. Combined with some good grammar instruction at the elementary-grade level, this foundation was good enough that my husband was invited to teach remedial college English as a sophomore, and I profited from this excellent early training all through school life. Our families were the key. Even then, it was years before we became aware of early speech errors, such as thinking that to take one for granted was "for granite" and keeping track of something was "keeping tract." It is easy not to think about the full meanings. Make it fun to speak good English. It is time for us all to be conscious of our voices, diction and word usage.

Our speech reveals that many of us have problems with hearing that we never recognized, although they did not necessarily result from deafness. Until at least age eight or nine, most children do not discriminate well in hearing sounds. That is the reason you should not normally expect children to pronounce all their words correctly until they are in that age range. Younger ones at four or five or even later often confuse such words as *got* and *caught* or *pie* and *by*. Or they come up with astonishing substitutes. One of our special friends, Angie Dutro, started all her words with *H*. Thus "I swim in my swimming suit" became "I him in my himming hoot."

Marty Hill, our little southern California neighbor, sensed that we liked six-year-olds, so he often came to visit us. One afternoon while I was cleaning our garage, he came by to show off his new jeans and to talk, as he often did, about his daddy.

"He's fixin' ernsmitz," he bragged with a childish attempt at nonchalance, thumbs in his pockets and wiggling his hips.

"Ernsmitz?" I asked.

"Yes, ernsmitz."

"You say, 'Ernsmitz'?" I tried futilely to respond so as not to embarrass Marty. He was a special friend, and I didn't want to spoil his story about his dad.

"Yes, ernsmitz. Don't you know?"

"No, Marty. I'm sorry I don't," I apologized.

"Of course you do," he derided.

"How does he use them?"

"He looks through 'em."

"Oh, you mean instruments!"

"Of course, ernsmitz. You knew all the time!"

Neither Marty's reasoning nor hearing was yet mature enough to understand my slowness. So you, too, will hear children earnestly singing in church, "Bringing in the cheese [sheaves]," or praying, "Our Father which art in heaven, Howard [hallowed] be Thy Name."

You will often find adults who have never learned to hear, and thus to pronounce, words correctly. They may say, for example, "I axed him," when they meant they "asked" him, or "I wanna take yer pitcher," instead of "I want to take your picture," or "reckunize" for *recognize*. *Duty* is commonly heard as "dooty" (instead of dyew-tee), *Tuesday* frequently as "Toosday" (instead of the proper Tyews-dy), and *err* is often pronounced "air" instead of "er."

Watch Your Grammar

Even in the media, few people are careful enough about their grammar, and *they* should be setting the standards. Many of them use singular verbs (predicates) with plural subjects, or vice versa. For example: "None of us are going." *None* (meaning "not one") is a singular subject, while *are* is a plural verb (predicate). *Us*—which is plural—is not the subject, but is simply the object of the preposition *of.* The correct sentence should be "None of us is going."

Try another example (this one *correct*): "All of us have parents." *All* is plural; *have* is plural. The subject *all* and the predicate *have* agree. A striking error that has recently been showing up with alarming frequency is the use of a subject pronoun when an object pronoun should have been employed. It is not "Our neighbors took my brother and *I* to the ball game," but "my brother and *me.*" *Me* is the object of the verb "took." We don't say, "Our neighbors took *I* to the ball game."

Many agree that our Hewitt-Moore grammar game not only helps their grammar but also makes grammar fun.[6] But more important, your students—and you—will become better understood and accepted persons. Your children's thoughtfulness for others, their manners, and how they listen will tell others how well you have educated them. They will be on their way to becoming skilled learners who will enjoy their education.

Teach Sounds of Letters (Phonics)

Another preparation for reading is sound-consciousness, sound discrimination, and the knowledge that words are made up of letters which have sounds. (This is briefly described in *Home-Grown Kids.*) Most folks are conscious these days of the value of phonics. Children need to be able to differentiate between sounds, although complete mastery of this should not be expected until they are fairly mature. Since their hearing is not highly discriminatory until they are eight or nine, articulation cannot be expected to be completely accurate until that age. Some children will know most common sounds as early as age three or four and will be able to discriminate between them as they grow older. Some sounds will be more difficult than others. Most parents do not need a system of phonics, though there are many good books on the market. You can use the things around you to teach sounds in an incidental way. One mother used the letters on cereal boxes. She would ask, "Do you hear the *O* in 'Cheerios'?" Another mother proceeded from a stop sign to *pop, cop, hop, mop, top,* and so on. Simply be sound-conscious.

Provide a mirror for yourself and your child when he reaches age four or five, so that he can watch how the tongue and teeth make different sounds. Play a little game in which you show him how you place your tongue, lips, and teeth—and let him look in the mirror and see how he places his own. This technique is often used for speech correction, but it is also good for the proper development of speech, which is closely associated with reading.

Many children I taught in remedial reading had not yet matured in hearing discrimination—partly because they had not had good models but mainly because they had not had any systematic training. Many of them had bad habits of speech and often did not pronounce words correctly, probably from copying their parents' speech. English teachers will tell you that it is almost impossible to change bad grammar habits if a student has learned bad usage at home as a young child, while children who have naturally learned good usage by parental example do very well in the study of grammar.

Make Labels

When your child is old enough to be interested in reading (or you want to get him interested in reading), make stick-on or pin-on labels for common household objects and have him play a game of putting them where they belong. Be sure you print them in what we call "manuscript" letters—which is the ordinary printing closest to book-type printing—not all block or capital letters. This style is illustrated on the opposite page. You might make labels for a chair, window, door, and maybe the refrigerator, for example. You don't even have to be restrictive about the length of the words. Tell the child what the word is, if necessary. Perhaps make a second label for "chair" and say, "Well, we have already put one out like this. Can you tell which one it is?" That's matching. Any kind of matching game with words or with other things—like textures of cloth, leaves, and so on—is good practice for helping children to see similarities and differences.

Make a Child's Journal

One of the best ways to start—even before using books—is to let your child dictate a story or an experience to you. You

a b c d e f
g h i j k l m
n o p q r s t
u v w x y z
A B C D E F G
H I J K L M N
O P Q R S T
U V W X Y Z

can do this for several weeks or months before you intend to proceed to books. Any time your child has something to tell you, write four or five sentences on a fairly large sheet of widely lined paper—something simple like "I went to the zoo today. I saw a camel. The camel had two humps. It was eating hay."

Help him keep a diary in a little notebook, so that he will have a collection of his own stories which he can read. From that you can help him see how other words relate to those in his story, like *zoo, too, moo, boo, goo,* and *coo;* or *hump, bump, lump, dump, pump, mumps, jump,* and *stump;* or *hay, may, bay, gay, jay, day, lay, stay, ray, pay, say,* and *way.* This is homemade phonics.

A Case in Point

With the simple program just described, many children will start to read to you all of a sudden. A typical instance is our little Indiana friend, who had immediate access to her mother for answers to her questions, was read to consistently from a very young age and participated in work, shopping, and the daily routine. At times her mother played little sound games with her, ran her finger from left to right under the lines as she read, and then discovered one day that Jill had picked out all the words that said "Jesus" on the page. When she was between six and seven, Jill found a stray first reader in the house (whose source the mother didn't even know) and started reading it. Then, as she went on reading everything she could get her hands on, including adult magazines, her mother had to limit her to fifteen or twenty minutes at a time, explaining that too much would hurt her eyes.

A nearby elementary school teacher, who had been watching this process and had some leanings toward home school, wanted to test her before she moved away. So, just before Jill turned eight, the parents reluctantly consented. Her reading tested at the seventh-grade level. The teacher had a good laugh over the fact that the parents, both college graduates, took the adult version of the test and came out at the ninth-grade level. We asked about other scores and found that Jill had rated at fourth-grade level on both math and spelling, having had nothing more than incidental attention to the practical aspects of math as used in the kitchen, and responses to her questions regarding sounds and words. The seventh-grade score is somewhat unusual but a third- or fourth-grade score happens often at ages seven and eight.

Even if a child does not show this particular behavior before age eight, a parent can usually have him ready for the third grade with only an hour a day of formal work for as little as six months. For instance, suppose his birthday is in January and you start your program then. By September, he will very likely be ready to go into the third grade. It may be hard to believe, but it is true.

I could tell you story after story in which children were nurtured in this manner, without pressure, and tested out from fourth- to ninth-grade reading level at age eight or nine. Their parents' only problem was to keep them developing in harmonious balance, rather than letting them become bookworms.

Now, don't feel bad if your child doesn't do all these things. He or she may just need more time. You will particularly find that boys need some extra time. Unless they have some abnormality, they will do well if you don't rush them! Rushing is one of the surest ways to destroy your home school—or any school.

Make learning to read as natural as learning to speak. Keep sound-consciousness (phonics) in all your conversations. Be thought-conscious, because you want to teach your child to read thoughtfully instead of being merely a repeater of words. Use reading as a stimulating experience for building character and skills and for meditation—and watch reading become fun!

8. Teaching Children to Think and Write Creatively

THE DEAN OF A leading university law school, a former college English professor, recently told us that many freshman law students must take remedial courses on how to write sentences and paragraphs. "They simply have not learned to express themselves clearly in speech or in writing," he said. This is not the first black wreath that has been hung over creative writing in recent years, for written communication has become a lost art over two generations. The fact is that these skills are largely neglected in our children's education.

We later asked an English and journalism professor how his freshman composition students were doing. He replied, "They not only can't write, they can't even think!" As we view the educational scene and hear such reports on the one hand, and watch the downward trend in the accomplishments of the schools on the other, we feel compelled to speak out. Some key causes of this dilemma are very clear. The conditions to which we expose our children generally deny them the opportunities to develop the arts of thinking and writing.

Why Can't Johnny and Jane Think Clearly?

1. *Rushing.* The first limitation is our hurry to start children into school. Youngsters less than eight or ten years of age are

not yet capable of hearing and reasoning clearly and consistently. They are gullible, readily believe what they see and hear, and are not fully able to sort out truth from error, right from wrong, or reality from fantasy. They not only accept the values of the other children who themselves are not yet carriers of good established social and moral habits, language and manners, but they also accept without discrimination what they read in the books placed before them and the events that they experience. Children in school generally have little opportunity to develop creative, independent thinking skills.

2. *Limited Adult Example and Responses.* Schoolchildren also have very limited access to their one adult model, the teacher, whom they imitate and look toward for responses. Teacher-student interaction is pitifully small compared to parent-child interaction in the home. Moreover, some teachers do not really understand how to stimulate thinking. By their very nature, most classrooms offer few chances for exploring, experimenting, setting goals, solving problems, making choices, questioning, and discussing. As a result, early exposure to conflicting values and the stifling effect of the average classroom rob the child of much of his normal development in logical and consistent thinking. Agatha Christie, who was home-schooled, stated in her autobiography that because children have things so completely arranged for them at school, they seem forlornly unable to produce their own ideas.

On the other hand, a one-to-one relationship with parents in the home allows for many activities and two-way conversations throughout the day, a process by which reasoning skills can be encouraged by precept and example on the basis of the parents' values. Those parents who attempt to justify a lack of such consistent daily responsiveness, by hoping to substitute "quality time" in the evening and on weekends, need to understand that *children do not usually learn best in concentrated doses.* What they need is a little here and a little there—freedom from pressure—with the literally hundreds of responses a child normally receives in a home as contrasted with the small number likely to be received in a classroom. Consistency and continuity of parental responses are jewels in rearing beautiful children. Usually this kind of home teaching will continue at least until the child is eight or ten, or even longer if the parents and children find this plan the best of the alternatives.

3. *Early Formalism.* Because reading affects one's thinking, a child who is forced to read formally before he can reason consistently (at about eight to twelve), whether at home or at school, is less likely to use his thinking powers to work out solutions, seek information by the discovery method, or invent ideas of his own. Often the quality of the material and the repetition necessary to teach a very young child to read are not really stimulating to his intellect. When his brain and senses are fully mature and integrated, the actual skill of learning to read thoughtfully is generally acquired with much less time and effort and he is soon able to handle more challenging material. Delaying formal book learning will give your child a chance to lay a firm foundation on which to build his superstructure of school-type education.

4. *Stifled Creativity.* In general, Western society has—by rushing children and forcing them through standardized curricula—virtually destroyed their creative potential. Some subjective estimates of "creativity" rate *average* individuals from ages twenty-five to sixty-five at 2 percent. They concede that a fifteen-year-old may have 12 percent and a twelve-year-old, 15 percent. But the creativity of the child at age five is appraised at 90 percent. These guesses are more likely right than wrong. How fortunate that Thomas Edison, George Washington Carver, and Cyrus McCormick had their basic school years at home!

As already noted, children need time to think—undisturbed and uncurbed by fixed subject lines. When you do ask questions, be patient and give them time to answer! The average ineffective teacher waits only a split second for an answer. Effective teachers wait at least four times as long. Great teachers often ask *why* and *how* questions for which they are willing to wait for answers as long as a year!

5. *The Workbook Syndrome.* Another deterrent in the develop-

ment of reasoning ability involves the methods used in teaching. When we asked the English professor what he thought caused the lack of thinking skills, he suggested that "workbooks reign in school, so the students spend much of their time just reading and regurgitating facts by filling in blanks and making canned choices—rather than developing their reasoning powers in discussing and evaluating materials, comparing one event with another, or gathering data from which to draw conclusions."

Many workbook questions require little or no thought. This dependence upon or overuse of workbooks appears to be just as pervasive in church schools as in public schools, and we have long been concerned about the problem. When teaching omits the essentials of constructive, original, thoughtful writing and speaking—using fewer *hows* and *whys* than *whats, wheres* and *whens*—it produces a dry, barren residue of education. The child may be absorbing factual knowledge but there is doubt about the wisdom and common sense which can be acquired with such methods. It may even be compared to the passive learning of television, which destroys the capacity for vigorous, connected thought. In a sense the brain is like a muscle and is strengthened with exercise. Passing facts through the mind onto paper without some mental exertion or application weakens the ability to think creatively and independently.

6. *Too Much Rote Learning.* Important as memorizing is, especially for gems of verse or mathematical facts, any teaching method which crowds the mind with knowledge, memorized bits of information, and others' opinions tends to discourage independent thought. Rather than applying his own powers of reason and judgment, a student who learns by rote can lose his capacity for discriminating between truth and error. He is then susceptible to the judgment and perception of others, and vulnerable to deception.

William Hazlitt, in an essay on learning, warns that too much reading at any age may cripple the mental powers. He says that the bookworm sees only the glimmering shadows of things reflected from the minds of others. Hazlitt points out that when the faculties of the mind are not exerted or when they are cramped by custom and authority, they become listless, torpid, and unfit for the purpose of thought or action.

Getting the Right "Early Start"

Let us start early to teach our children how to speak and think and write. As parents, begin at the baby's birth by talking to him and encouraging his efforts to mimic you by shaping his lips and making little sounds. Give him plenty of opportunity to express himself as his speech becomes more fluent, helping him to organize his thoughts and form complete sentences. In a very subtle and indirect way, you can teach him to use words correctly and to increase his vocabulary, helping him with questions or suggestions to tell events in sequence. Take care not to be "preoccupied" when he wants to tell about the unusual bird he saw in the back yard or what happened when he went with Daddy to the store. Encourage him to retell you the stories you have read to him or suggest that he tell them to others.

To develop his thinking skills, encourage the child to plan, initiate, and create some of his own activities. Don't be too quick to supply answers to all his questions or yield to the temptation to tell him before he asks. Instead, help him discover his own answers or give him time to think of ways to solve his problems. He might even come up with several solutions from which to choose.

If you have your children memorize Scripture texts or other verses, help them understand the meanings and get them to explain them in their own words. In fact, when a child is old enough to express himself adequately, do not assume that he has really learned *any* concept until he is able to express the idea in his own words.

In short, try to strike a happy balance between helping your child and imposing your own solutions on him. Providing ready-made knowledge may prevent him from discovering information for himself. Even if his trial-and-error methods seem to waste time, you must remember that he may be learning more than one thing while he is experimenting. Stimulate and stretch his mental powers by helping him to contemplate what could have been done differently to improve a certain course of events, how one should act in a similar situation, or what would have happened if the circumstances had been changed.

Applying Principles in a Practical Way

Encourage your child to apply to his own life the knowledge he gains: what he can learn from others' mistakes, what principles can be used in a practical way, and what he should try to change in his habits or lifestyle to accomplish the most good for himself and others.

Some of the practical skills which should be taught as needed are: How to fill out a job application and résumé, how to write a business letter, how to balance a checkbook, how to understand written directions for the use of appliances, how to fill out such reports as income tax returns, and so on.

It is important to provide practical work, begun as soon as the child can walk, continued appropriately for his age, and balanced in equal amounts with study when he reaches the age for formal schooling. Such activity, guided by proper instruction and supervision, develops observational powers and the ability to plan and execute, as well as logical thinking. It also helps to develop such character qualities as perseverance, orderliness, neatness, dependability, and diligence—along with mature self-direction, self-discipline, and independent reasoning.

Developing Creative Writing

When your child has become quite fluent in speaking (around age five, six, or seven), it is time to put down his ideas on paper. Since the actual mechanics of writing are still too difficult for him, this is the time when stories, letters, or a diary of special activities may be dictated by the child and recorded by the parent. Such dictation is an excellent method for communicating with a faraway grandparent, as well as for recording events for posterity. At first, it is wise to make it fun and make it short. Here are suggested steps:

1. Begin with some activity which you and your child or family enjoy. For example, it could be making popcorn, a trip to the zoo, a train ride, feeding the ducks or the sea gulls at the beach.
2. While you are involved in the activity, talk about how much fun it would be to write down a description of what you have done.
3. When you complete your activity and the memories of the experience are still fresh in your child's mind, have him tell about it as if he were telling it to someone who wasn't there, such as Grandma. This will be harder for some children than others, and it may help to have him say the words as if he had just arrived at Grandma's or Aunty's home. As soon as he starts talking, begin writing. Never mind if it isn't perfect, and give him time to formulate his thoughts although you may suggest alternate ways of expression if what he says is really off the track, or help him form his sentences if he has difficulty. But be sure you let it be his story, not yours. This is like painting from life instead of coloring within the lines in a coloring book.
4. As soon as he has finished, read the story back to him. Pointing to each word will help to develop his concept of "words." Keep the story in permanent form as in a booklet so that it can be read over and over again.

Variations of such a diary or collection of short stories may include:

1. Preparing a separate booklet of trip experiences to which you can add snapshots taken while traveling.
2. Making a scrapbook of pressed flowers. Under each flower, record when and where you found the flower before it is pressed so that the page is ready for the flattened flower.

For a professional-looking specimen, smooth a sheet of clear contact paper over the flower.

3. Let your child illustrate each dictated story with his own creative artwork.

Encouraging Communication Skills

When your child starts formal schooling, whether in a regular or home school, don't forget the importance of these communication skills. Be sensible and balanced in your teaching. Don't throw out all the workbooks, but use them wisely. Take the opportunity to have the child discuss what has been read, not only identifying the facts, but interpreting what the author meant. Then, of course, he may do a workbook page, but not necessarily every page. Also encourage your child to apply what has been learned to his own experience—either to solve a problem, incorporate an idea into his own life, or relate it to helping someone or fixing something, e.g., loading a dishwasher or repairing a switch.

Continue to provide opportunities for both oral and written expression. The pen is still mightier than the sword. Almost any normal child can excel in this area if given deserved attention by someone who can teach it. Such diligence will pay off when your child enters or returns to school and/or goes on to college. When a child prepares a report for science or social studies, never allow him to copy the material verbatim, but insist that he digest the information and put it into his own words. Give him lots of practice in paraphrasing both oral and written material.

A parent of one student who had been home-schooled since the seventh grade and is now enrolled in college, told of her daughter's experience in her first English class. She observed that creative writing is often not emphasized enough in the usual home-school curriculum. Even though her daughter had always done well when tested on the mechanics of English, she lacked practice in applying the rules and on a recent paper lost a full grade point because of neglect in placing commas and checking spelling.

This is a warning to all concerned parents: include oral and written expression for your child. You should not consider your children educated until they are proficient in communication skills and also have good penmanship. But you cannot expect to teach these skills in a short time! The earlier you start—once your child is sufficiently mature—and the more consistent you are, the more thorough a job you can do. The quality of education you impart will be judged largely by those very obvious skills as they are later used in college, in business, and in everyday life.

9. Using Illustrations That Fascinate Minds and Hearts

ABOVE ALL OTHERS, I remember one church leader of my childhood. I could hardly wait for his next visit. He was president of the local church conference and, by all normal standards, we kids had no reason to expect much from an administrator and theologian. He was not supposed to be a "kids' preacher," yet he had a secret or two that more preachers and teachers should learn. First, he told many stories, and they were always to the point. They were like big bay windows, letting in the light and lessons through rose-colored glass, always making the colors more vivid. Second, he wrapped his heart around us; he was more concerned about how well we understood than how much of a reputation he had to make.

Pastor Broderson—for that was the man's name—had mastered the art of illustration. He had learned to see a story in everything from a toothpick to a threshing machine, from a teaspoon and teacup to the Rose Bowl, from the tiniest bug to the biggest elephant, and from a few grains of sand to the constellation Orion. Furthermore, he made each story personal, often drawing its lessons from our daily experiences and immediate surroundings or from his own. He did not need a book of "illustrations"—although these may often serve a good purpose—and he did not have to stretch the details in order to make his point.

Pastor Broderson had also learned how to avoid self-consciousness. He had discovered that the more you are thinking of others and their needs, concerned for their present or eternal welfare, the less likely you are to be worried about yourself, your abilities or the way you might appear to others. This is the secret of self-worth, of being valued and sensing that you are needed for a purpose beyond your own selfish interests. It is also the way to make your lessons clear. Such friendly people make great teachers, and we do well to follow their model in both the home school and the institution. Love your children more than yourself—and see the world through *their* eyes.

Tell Stories with Imagination

A good teacher not only sees a story in everything, but also tells it as simply and actively as possible. This often requires more imagination than triggering the illustration in the first place. Such imagination will be productive only as you are understanding of the developmental needs of your youngsters. For example, you will avoid telling a five- or six-year-old child stories which require consistent reasoning ability to appreciate. And you will have to use special care when you tell an inner-city child stories about the farm or when you describe to a rural youngster the goings-on in the ghetto.

In any event, a lively imagination is a powerful teaching tool. Cultivate it. Ask questions for your own and your children's information. Intersperse them throughout your story, especially when you are teaching little children. Remember to emphasize the *whys* and *hows*. And if you want to insure greater learning, be sure to give your young listeners time to answer your questions. The longer this interval (within reason), the deeper will be the thoughtfulness of response.

Don't neglect detail in your story. It excites the imagination of the children and colors their mental picture. You may be counting the legs on a spider or whiskers on a cat. You may be describing the cockpit of an airliner or the stalking attack of a jungle tiger. In the latter case, tell how the tiger lifted one paw slowly and then another; how he stopped for a moment to sniff the air; how he could see right through the dark; then how he stepped on a dry twig which made a crackling sound. Such details not only appeal to the senses—touch, smell, vision, hearing—but also develop suspense.

Although not all stories can readily be adapted to suspense, this tool is certainly crucial to effective teaching when your illustration goes beyond a few words of analogy. Stories which delay revealing their outcome bring an aura of mystery that attracts nearly all ages. However, even simple analogy can be colorful—as, for example, when you report that "the horse ran as if he was scared," or that "the little boy climbed trees as fast as a monkey." Using analogies gives life to your teaching and with a little effort they may become a natural part of your conversation.

Teach with Enthusiasm and Animation

As your teaching becomes more enthusiastic, and therefore more interesting and exciting, you yourself will become a more fascinating person to your children. You are potentially your own best visual aid, but don't hesitate to use any dignified audiovisual technique or demonstration that makes your point. Such aids may include puppets, flannelgraphs, magazine pictures, household tools, kitchen utensils, or even your fingers. You may also include almost any kind of music that is soft and melodious, including your own singing.

Don't hold yourself back. Become a more lively person in all your activities, although not necessarily trying to be a clown. Don't be afraid to use your eyes (big as dollars) or your hands (like little people) or your smile or a thousand other forms of body language. Again, wrap your heart around your listeners; your self-consciousness will fade and your animation will captivate.

Stretch Mind Power with Questions

Don't forget to raise questions. Keep your children's minds "on the stretch." Your curiosity will nourish theirs, especially as they grow into more reasoning creatures. You will never completely eliminate the *whats, wheres, whens,* and *how muches,* but by stressing the *whys* and *hows,* you, too, will develop a genuine curiosity and will generate the same in your youngsters. Combined with reasonable self-control, this curiosity can yield brilliance.

Many effective tools are available for illustrations. With only a little thought and planning, you will likely become a favored storyteller if you use

—personal experiences or experiences of which you have close knowledge.

—contrasts, whether in voice tone or descriptions—such as shades of sunset or animal sounds.

—recency, whether in the immediate or near past.

—familiarity, for familiar things make the best "learning hooks" for new information.

—heroism or good, principled deeds, even sacrificial acts.

—tenderness, as in the story of William Tell or with animal stories such as Mary's Lamb (both in the Moore-McGuffey Readers), and other parent-child, brother-sister relationships or pet-care illustrations.

—positive lessons which tend to uplift.

—suspense or mystery, used in a constructive way.

—secrets, for children of all ages love them.

Practice makes perfect in using these techniques. Be deliberate. Try them, and you will soon become a natural storyteller. Experiment and know the satisfaction of having made your point—the well-earned mark of a good teacher.

10. Getting the Most from Test-Taking and Test-Making

ONE OF THE MOST fun things of our lives has been telling scared students how to perform well on standardized tests. In 1967, three black girls from Detroit came to our Hinsdale, Illinois, home when we headed an advanced study center in connection with the University of Chicago. They had been home schooled because their father, a Detroit factory worker, had feared for their physical and spiritual safety in the local system. Since their mother used no special curriculum, the girls felt like Topsys— "out of the swim" of modern educational patterns. One sister wanted to be a nurse, another a teacher, another a minister's wife, but all felt they "could never make it." We advised them to take the General Education Development test (GED), but they were positive they wouldn't score well.

Nevertheless, we gave them some hints on how to take a test and encouraged them to study for a few days. All three passed high on the GED, and the last we heard, had become college graduates: one a nurse, one a college dean of women, and one a minister's wife!

It is possible that even a good student who is careless about test-taking may receive a *D* or an *F* or do poorly on a standardized achievement or intelligence test. This happened one day to a group of highly skilled math students in a college we administered. The teacher was unusually well qualified and was reasonable in his grading criteria. But in cramming for finals, the men had stayed up most of the night. By class time the vital current which flowed from their bodies to their brains was at such low ebb that they could not recall what they actually knew. When the professor found what had happened, he gave a new test, and nearly all received high grades.

Students need help on how to take tests and how to study for them. Before a test is given, the teacher should explain exactly what is expected. Unfortunately, many teachers are not sure. Or there may be so many unanticipated possibilities for answers that students are confused. This is the result of poor test-making, something that happens far too often. If an objective, standardized test is used, it is only fair to explain to the student how the test can best be handled.

Test-Taking Tips

People may as often pass or fail on *how* they take tests as on what they know. The following principles apply equally to the child taking an elementary-level periodic test in language, math, or social studies and to the adult student taking a medical school examination, a Federal Service Entrance Examination (FSEE), or a Law School Aptitude Test (LSAT).

Prepare your body to be in the best possible physical condition so that your mind can operate to its fullest potential. Here are six important steps:

1. Plan ahead so as to be fully rested. Do not overload your schedule just before test time.
2. Be as relaxed as possible, realizing that you can likely take the test a second time if necessary.
3. Make sure to get plenty of sleep the night before the test, preceded by thorough and physically sound exercise—fast walking, cycling, running, swimming, for example.
4. Don't go into an examination with a full stomach. Perhaps the best time for most people to take a test is in the morning when food is well-digested and vitality is at its peak—either before breakfast or an hour or so before noon. It is usually

better to have eaten fresh fruit and grains than such food
as starchy vegetables, meat, or eggs, which take two to three
times as long to digest as the former. The brain needs the
fresh and abundant supplies of blood which otherwise might
be helping to digest the stomach's overload of food.

5. Drink as much water as you can reasonably manage. The
idea may seem strange, but water actually does help "lubri-
cate the brain," with its many contacts through which the
electric current of sound learning and memory must pass.
Water also washes away poisons that might otherwise tend
to intrude on body health and thought processes.

6. Be well prepared both in terms of having taken care of
restroom needs and having brought all necessary supplies,
such as pencils, paper, or other required tools.

In the matter of actual test-taking, the factor of time is all-
important. Determine right at the start whether a time limit has
been set for completing the test. If it has, go through the test
thoroughly but rapidly, answering all of the questions you know
for sure. Then go back over the test and answer those questions
about which you have some doubt or need more time to think
through. Don't let your worry or delay over difficult questions
keep you from getting to those which you could have done quickly
and easily. Following this procedure is crucial for high scoring
on timed objective tests and desirable on essay examinations as
well.

In doing an essay test, it is usually a good idea to jot down
a brief outline at the beginning of your answer, and then to
follow this outline all the way through. Organizing in this way
will help you express your ideas clearly and keep you from wan-
dering away from the subject under discussion.

For many tests, such as entrance tests for law and medical
schools, the Graduate Record Examination (GRE), college entrance, and the GED, there are manuals that give details and
include previous tests. Careful study of these usually (not always)
familiarizes the examinee with the peculiarities of the tests. These
are helpful in several respects: the student is generally not so
fearful of the unknown; he knows the instructions well and so

saves time in reading them again; and he is alert to the potential traps. Professional teachers are increasingly teaching to such tests, even in grade school. We don't necessarily recommend this, for it sets up the test as your standard and your limitation. Yet, if other teachers are doing it in schools around you, you may feel forced to do it too.

Fairness in Grading

We make no suggestion here about specific marking systems—whether to grade by percentage or alphabet, by marking satisfactory–unsatisfactory or pass–fail. We have no preference, but we do point to a key principle in such marking: be fair. Where there is any question, give the student the benefit of the doubt. To the extent that our emotions or biases are allowed to enter into our grading—and this often happens—we are judging wrongfully. For one human being to undertake to evaluate another is a serious matter.

The variables are so numerous, so let us be respectful, even reverent, as we undertake this task. For example, a child may have problems of vision or hearing or any one of a hundred neurological anomalies. Or he may come from an unsettled or broken home and be in no emotional condition to do his best or to compete with those of his own ability. Or he may be working in a language with which he is not very familiar. Or a teenage girl may be going through unobservable trauma during her menstrual cycle. A married student may be having domestic problems, and another student may be experiencing deep concern over a sick relative or an emotional loss in courtship. And you, at least half-blind to all of these factors, may be appraising them with little thought for their personal handicaps! Practice the Golden Rule.

Some subjects—as in medical or law school, or such vocational instruction as aircraft-engine repair—demand a certain standard knowledge of technical details. In such subjects the students must be graded against a well-established set of criteria and not passed or certificated until they have mastered these basics. This is quite different from grading on general education where students are often judged against a "normal curve," that is, the average of other human beings, instead of a clearly measurable set of standards.

Seldom, if ever—even in nontechnical subjects—is it wise to grade by the normal curve. Saint Paul once wrote to the Corinthians: "They measuring themselves by themselves . . . are not wise." [1] While it may comfort some when the "average" performance deteriorates, the standard then becomes unstable. In fact, it is *never* stable. This is precisely what is happening in many educational circles today. A reasonable standard should be set for giving a grade (if a grade must be given), and everyone who reaches that standard should be rewarded with the best grade. It is conceivable that in an inspired or highly selected class most of the students could receive *A*'s.

Good Teachers Make Good Students

To the extent that students know (or do not know) how to take tests, they often pass or fail, reflecting either glory or discredit on their parents, teachers, and their schools. We have presented the foregoing material to help you, the teacher, give your students the best opportunity to show how soundly they have been taught the basic principles of the subject matter you have presented. We have used these techniques with thousands of students in preparing them for the GED, LSAT, FSEE, Medical Aptitude, and similar tests, and, as with the three black sisters whose experience was related at the beginning of this chapter, we have shared an almost universal experience of happy, sometimes unexpected success.

Finally, never test any person unless he is ready mentally, physically, and emotionally. This includes young children who must not be subjected to tests of skills or reasoning ability which is beyond their maturity. Few children are ready for standardized achievement testing before ages eight to ten.

11. How, When, and Where for Your Child to Study Easiest and Best

ONE OF THE MOST frustrating experiences for a teacher, either in the home or in the school, is to have a student who is not systematic and does not know how to study. This deficiency may grow out of a home situation if the child is at school, or out of a school situation if the child is also studying at home. It is well to consider how to help our students study, instead of creating situations in which we somehow contrive to make certain that they *can't* study. Seldom in recent years have we found a high-school study hall or a college-dormitory study hour which clearly protected the sanctity of the student's study time. Yet the student's study habits have a lot to do with *your* success as a teacher.

Few students know naturally how to be systematic. Few organize to plan their work and work their plans. Yet this goal, when well learned, is greater than the sum of a year's classes in most schools. As a teacher, set an example for your students. Teach them to make a list of the things they are going to do each day and to check off each one as it is accomplished, transferring the leftovers to another list for the next day. Teach them to keep a daily schedule and a monthly and yearly calendar. A daily journal, one of the most helpful tools, can be kept quite simply on a calendar of the type that has a space for each day. These are often given away at local stores. Otherwise, one can buy or make a little book in which to write.

Teach your students to avoid the general futility and absurdity of cramming. Below are a few hints on how to study. As you go over these hints with your students, help them to understand that, in the enterprise of study, their success or bankruptcy will largely depend upon them alone.

Building a Successful Study Cycle

Plan your work. Both you and your students should make a reasonable schedule, budget your time, and try to stay within your budget. Use a calendar and make out a time chart, but use it wisely. You become its master, not its slave! Schedule hours for classes and for leisure or outside work. Schedule hours of study for the next class.

The best time to study is usually before meals, and the least productive time is after the evening meal, when the body and brain are tired and the stomach is usually full. (The very best time to study is before breakfast. Some authorities say this time is worth three to five times as much as the time after supper.)

One of the best ways to be sure you are fresh and ready to study is to have had good food, a sound sleep, and plenty of exercise. The most productive sleep time is *before midnight.* World authorities on circadian rhythms say that these natural "clocks" time your body as they time the tides of the sea. [1] For genuine rest, the sleep before the midnight hour is worth two to three times as much as the time after midnight. Many people insist that they are "night creatures," yet the circadian principle applies to all of us, and to the extent to which we violate that principle, we are likely to suffer ill health, neurosis, or early death.

Remember that mental health includes self-discipline. Both physical and mental health must be considered crucial if your students are to get the most out of their studies. This means not only regularity in eating, drinking plenty of water, sleeping soundly, exercising, and in other health-building habits—and attending to illnesses as soon as you recognize them—but also means understanding mental health as a key factor in successful living, both in school and out. The average student with better-than-average effort and personal discipline will get along much better than a "gifted" child without that self-control. Discipline is not only the fine art of discipleship, but also a key to genius. This means that a student should be discouraged from dodging principles or facts, thus learning to meet his problems calmly and squarely. He will find that procrastination—forever putting things off—is the thief of time. He will discover that dreaming is not doing and wishing is not producing. This is why we insist on a balance in education—physical, mental, social, and spiritual. This kind of balance eliminates worry, because there is a plan. You guide your students to work on it, using their hands to develop self-respecting manual skills. Student and teacher are self-directed and know where they are going.

Set aside a place for study. Each student should have a definite place for studying. If possible, designate it as *only* for this purpose, so that when he goes there he has a feeling for study. For some this should not be near a bed nor a stereo! In boarding schools, a roommate can be either a blessing or a handicap. Wherever possible, ensure that your students are relatively free from interruption in a well-ventilated room, more cool than warm, and with adequate light that does not shine directly into their eyes. Try to have all unnecessary things out of the way, and all the material needed for the day's lesson at hand, particularly a good dictionary. Get the best kind of notebooks, paper, pencils, or other equipment for specific studies.

Get down to the job. Encourage the student to begin studying the moment he sits down. His goal should be to concentrate on what he is doing—not dreaming, but working with intensity while he works. Later on, he can play intensely while he plays. Motivation is vital here. If the studies are meaningful to the student, so that he can see them taking him somewhere, he will develop a deeper, "intrinsic" interest. Encourage him to read as widely as possible on the subject at hand.

Learn to read efficiently. Give your students help on how to read effectively, but don't burden them with guilt if they don't read every word of every assignment. Many school assignments are little more than busy work. Oftentimes, students are bored because they have already known the material for months or even years. And while we don't endorse lazy bones, we suggest that there is usually no great virtue in hasty or "speed" reading.

Yet, reading is extremely important for sound scholarship. Lazy reading can take hours, where careful, efficient readers can absorb more material in minutes. Here are several principles you can teach your students:

1. Have a definite goal when you start to read. Glance over the table of contents, paragraph headings, illustrations, the prelude or summary of a chapter—to get an idea about what you are going to read. Develop some questions in your mind. Think of the author and also of your teacher. Relate the material to other things you have already learned and plan to learn. It will often help if you will "recite" to yourself.

2. Make yourself aware of technical terms. Look up in the dictionary words that are difficult for you. Verify their meaning, and also their *spelling and pronunciation.* Many people have problems with spelling and often become confused with sounds. Don't be afraid of new words. Keep a record of them and use them several times so that you feel comfortable with them. Leading executives have generally been found to have superior vocabularies.

3. Read without lip movement and without using your fingers to follow the words. Read silently and rapidly, reaching forward in the paragraph rather than lazing back. Occasionally practice reading against time, although *speed reading* is doubtful practice for serious material. Concentration is the key to reading, which in turn is an active process. Your alertness and your curiosity will make a great deal of difference in how much you learn.

Practice remembering. The key principle here is that remembering follows understanding. Encourage your students to form rich associations about the things they want to keep in mind. For example, when they read about the Battle of Dunkirk, if they realize the distance across the English Channel is about the same as from their farm into town, they can more easily remember that historical event.

Foreign-language specialists say that you must train your ear by speaking aloud the sentences you read and write when you are learning a new language. We would add to this that you should try to speak those languages with the exact intonations of the native people. When we lived in Japan, we often went out and walked with the people in the markets and talked with them so as to learn their precise sounds. It was fun later when we talked with Japanese strangers over the phone to have them think that we were Japanese. Do your best to *think* in a new language you may be learning. You will soon be surprised to find that you will be using words in that language instead of your own native tongue. When that time comes, you will realize that you are getting up and over the language hill.

Reviewing is also important for remembering. "Repetition strengthens associations" is a stark truism. And the stronger the associations, the better your memory will be. It has also been found that if you review at increasingly longer intervals—at first a few hours after you study, then a few days, then a few weeks—you will learn that lesson unusually well. A student probably cannot do this for every lesson, but this will make sense for important items.

Take good notes. Whatever else you do, teach your students to write notes clearly, legibly. Make sure that your own penmanship is good and your thoughts blend well. Keep notes on each subject together with your students. Whenever you use an outline form—which is generally best—we recommend that you use complete sentences. If a student takes good notes and then reviews them at the intervals suggested, he will undoubtedly do well. Yet generally speaking, don't go overboard in insisting on a lot of note-taking. If one has to make a choice, remember that it is more important to think!

Writing Papers

When you or your children are writing papers or long items for your diary, remember several points: record those things that (a) are of particular interest to you; (b) can be covered in the time allotted; (c) are worth writing about; (d) are important to justify using your time; and (e) may be of future use. Make an outline of what you want to write about. If possible, approach the topic from some special angle. This allows for some real creativity and will make writing a much more valuable experience. Be very accurate in quoting from other sources. Be particularly careful in quoting from a newspaper or magazine article that is already quoting a study. This use of "secondary sources" can be like a game of "gossip" with all its funny—and sometimes tragic—fallout. The original study or an additional source should be consulted whenever possible. Encourage students to begin writing soon enough to have their papers prepared before they are due.

Use good grammar. Teach your students by example. Know what you want to say and line up your thoughts in an orderly way. Be yourself. Be truthful. Keep your writing lively. Use appropriate words—language that is pure and kind and true, the outward expression of an inward grace.

12. Remotivating a Burned-Out Child

WE RECENTLY received a letter from a Midwestern mother of four. She was angry at the schools for a "sloppy" job of education, at society for insisting on such schools, at herself for being so ignorant and gullible about the educational process—and at us for not warning her about the possible home problems and protests when you take your youngsters out of school. The facts were: (1) we have had few, if any, negative reactions from children who have been removed from these institutions and no previous complaints from parents who removed them; (2) we have often warned about peer pressure and loss of respect for parents by youngsters who were put out of the home and institutionalized at early ages; (3) we write our books to help parents *avoid* gullibility and ignorance; and (4) indeed we do need to say more on how to offset childish doubts about home school and about Mom as teacher.

Teaching your child at home is really very simple if you start early and start right. We are delighted when we get letters from parents with very young children who are already laying a strong foundation for optimum learning as described in *Home-Grown Kids.*

Of course, parents will have a harder row to hoe when they have long neglected their garden. Whether consciously or not, they looked the other way while the weeds grew, and now must

112

dig much deeper to get them out by the roots. The business of retraining burned-out and peer-dependent children often does cause pain and demand greater effort than required from families who have not surrendered their little ones early to institutions. Yet even parents who must overcome this handicap will find the effort well worthwhile. Most children who are helped to understand why parents often make the greatest teachers (see chapter 3), who are made officers in family "corporations" or industries (see chapter 13) and allowed to help in their management, will in a surprisingly short time become supportive heirs and overcome their bad habits of griping, dawdling, carelessness and general nonsense.

We hope suggestions given here will make your first year easier, though there is no instant cure for the accumulation of school-induced difficulties. These "problems" are not necessarily listed in order of importance:

Problem #1: Motivation

"My children are tired of school and couldn't care less whether they learn or not. School is a necessary evil as far as they are concerned. It seems like pure laziness to me, but is there any hope of renewing their zest for learning? Our little one at five has a beautiful curiosity and desire to learn."

There are two basic kinds of motivation, *extrinsic* and *intrinsic.* Extrinsic motivation relies on an outside source to produce a certain accomplishment—a star for good work or a treat for dinner. This is a justifiable method, but is more shallow and often less effective than intrinsic motivation, which comes from within the child and is inherent in the activity itself. For example, the act of swinging is fun so children return again and again to the swing for the sheer joy of it. They like to make cookies or bread because they get satisfaction from playing in the dough, making something to eat, surprising someone, or just being your partner in work. Or they might be motivated to read when they are old enough because they need to follow a recipe by themselves, or learn to weld so that they can help repair an old car.

Your task as home teacher is to make the classwork and all learning for your children of such a challenging and exciting nature that they will want to return to it again and again. The following points will help you make such motivation happen:

1. Remember that learning is fun if you are achieving and very seldom making errors. If the work is a struggle and your child is making many mistakes, it is likely that the material is yet ahead of him, or is being presented in segments that are too large or too difficult for him to comprehend. This is a special danger with correspondence or workbook courses which require endless hours of solo work. Either break down the work into smaller units of information or change to simpler material.

2. Compliment the quality of your child's work whenever possible. Praise for work well done (more than the praising of your child himself) tends to build vital self-worth rather than ego pride. Foster a desire to achieve and to perform all work at the highest level of his or her ability. Help your child to realize that even an ordinary mind, when well-disciplined, will reach higher levels than the most highly educated mind and greatest talents that lack self-control.

3. Be positive in your manner, even when correction is needed. If you are tempted to make a negative comment, stop to think how you might turn it into a constructive suggestion. Seek never to bring discouragement to your child. For example, instead of saying, "You are making mistakes," tell the child, "This is a really neat-looking letter, but I do see two words misspelled. Do you think you can find them and correct them? Then you can send it to Aunt Susan."

4. Insist, *we repeat,* on perfection (as measured at the child's individual maturity) at each step, but only on small units. Once a page has been read perfectly, do not expect the child to read that one perfectly *again* in conjunction with another page. Remember—if your child could do all his work perfectly, he would not need school. Expect that there will be some mistakes, and seek to capitalize on them in positive ways.

5. Give prompt feedback whenever possible. Research has

shown that far more learning takes place when you correct written work "on the spot." Such supervised study has been shown to be far more effective than rote homework. If it is all right, tell the child so, perhaps marking it E for "excellent." If one or two items are wrong, help him to reason out the right answer, and to change it so that the entire page or unit is correct. Encourage the child to think his work through, without belittling or scolding in any way. Then give him an "O.K." when all the mistakes have been corrected. This will eliminate *ABC*-type grades, because all work will eventually be correct. End-of-the-quarter, or end-of-the-year grades can be "Excellent" or "Satisfactory," if you and your child have done your best. Whether a child succeeds or fails at home or school, his teacher shares the praise or blame.

6. Include children in the planning of subjects, projects, trips, and the investigation of and decision about a cottage industry. They will then have more enthusiasm and cooperate better. Make them officers in the family "business." Have them count the money earned and spent and keep accounts. Parents who have been home-schooling for some time almost always report growth in family togetherness and a mutual sense of each child's importance as a member of the family team.

7. Set small, immediate goals in addition to long-term ones. Children need to see the results of their work each day. The younger children especially do not yet have the capacity to wait a long time for evidence of their accomplishments.

8. If your child dawdles, you may have to try more than one corrective. If the first doesn't work, try another. Begin by making sure the work is neither too hard nor too extensive. Try using a stopwatch or timer and having the child race against time. Or tell him that if he gets the first five (or ten) answers perfectly, he doesn't have to do the rest. You might provide the incentive of a special activity or a shortened school day if he finishes the assigned task on time. Be sure to have the children show Daddy and/or others their work. Have a bulletin board for excellent work.

Problem #2: Doubts about Your Qualifications

Your children think you are not qualified. They say, "You're not a real teacher. Mrs. Smith never made us do that."
After all, you are Mom! And few educators, not to mention children, realize that the greatest basic education comes not from institutions but from inspired parents and other interested adults. Just answer something like this: "That's interesting. Did you know that parents have been proven by research studies to be the super teachers for their own children? Thomas Edison was taught by his mother and he became the greatest inventor in history." Then let them look up some of the things he was responsible for—the electric light bulb, phonograph, motion picture camera and projector, among hundreds of other things. Go on to tell them about other famous people schooled at home. (See list in Appendix C.)

Problem #3: Justifying the Writing "Basics"

"Why do I have to spell it right? This is history, not spelling."
Such a response is brought about by failure to integrate school subjects with real life. Written work in any subject should be done in your child's best penmanship and be accurate in punctuation, grammar, and spelling. Help him to understand that we study spelling in order to express ourselves effectively in writing.
If a child has written a composition, letter or report, you may need to help him correct (edit) it and then have him recopy it. Explain that people who write books or articles for magazines and newspapers often have to edit or rewrite their material several times before the article is published. Teach him to look up unknown words in the dictionary and check facts in an encyclopedia. (You may have to do this often, yourself.) Tell him that high school and college teachers usually count off one point for each spelling or punctuation error, and that grades count when it comes to being accepted for specialized training or for a job. Compare such an error to leaving out an important ingredient in a recipe such as salt in a stew.

Besides, you're the teacher now and, because you love your child, you are training him to do *everything* to the best of his ability. Most children practice hammering pegs and then nails before they learn how to do carpentry, and it would be about as futile to try to build a brick wall without knowing how to mix mortar as to write a composition without good grammar.

Problem #4: Poor Penmanship

"My child has terrible penmanship and forms his letters incorrectly."

Get a good beginning penmanship book, such as the Palmer Method, and start from scratch—but tell the child that he can do less practice if he does a letter or assignment well the first time or two. Take a sample of his handwriting of a special quotation before he starts this procedure, and then do another about once a month to compare and note the improvement. Help him take pride in his writing. Try it on yourself, too. We all slip a little as time goes by.

Problem #5: Carelessness

"My child really doesn't care if he makes mistakes or not—just so he gets it done and can hand it in."

This is the result of a former teacher's failure to follow through. An error checked as wrong, but never corrected, does not promote learning. Even in a test, a child should know what he missed and why. Just putting down a right answer is not enough either. He should have to find the answer or learn how to find it, and only when the answers are correct is the paper considered complete. Treatment of this problem may be almost as painful as surgery, but just as necessary to bring a cure. Immediate rewards of "100%" or "Excellent" for a perfect paper will encourage a child to be more careful and to check it *before* handing it in.

Problem #6: Dictionary Phobia

"I hate looking words up in the dictionary."

Do you have a small dictionary handy—perhaps at arm's reach? Has your child really learned how easy it is when he knows how to use the guide words at the top of the pages? Try having a dictionary drill to practice finding a word quickly. Develop a word-consciousness. Play word games like Scrabble. Help him understand the abbreviations as explained in the front of the dictionary and even how the word was derived, if he is mature enough for this. Tell him that most executives know many words.

Problem #7: The "I-Hate-Reading" Complaint

"My child is a poor reader and just hates it."
More than likely, your child started formal schooling too young and was not yet ready to handle the task of reading. He has not had enough success experiences and is burned out by too much pressure. You must use some different methods.
1. First, give him a rest—over the summer is often adequate—but continue to read to him. Bring in incidental reading in a *different* context than school—nature or Bible games with a few simple words which would be within his ability. If he has memorized Scripture, help him find the verses in a large-print Bible. Tell him the first few words and have him read a verse through—not as a "reading class" but just incidentally, perhaps as part of worship time. Of course, he can "read" it because he already had it in his head. All he has to do is to transfer that to the printed word. We think there is a special blessing in that.
2. Present only material with which your child can have success, moving only as fast as he can achieve. A child should test two to three grades *above* his actual grade level in order to handle his daily lessons well. Try to find material a grade or two *below* the level at which your child tests, and take it from a *different* reading series than the one used previously.
3. If your child does not easily comprehend what he reads, note his "decoding" ability (sounding out words). If he can't really *read* the words, he will not understand the material. He may need a thorough rerun through a phonics program, or at least enough to fill in the gaps he probably missed when not ready.
4. If he still does not understand the material, try having him read it aloud, to see if he understands it when he reads *to* you.

Some children need to *hear* the material, and verbalizing it in any way possible is sometimes helpful.

5. If this does not help, talk about it together. Try *simpler* or *shorter* segments.

6. When your child falters, repeats words, and so on, *slow him down.* Have him read by sounds, imitating a slowed-down record. Have him "march through" the sounds and syllables. After reading this way for a while, let him speed up a little. If the reading begins faltering again, *slow him down once more.* Sometimes it helps to read this way right along with him. Then drop your voice away, bringing it back in if there is still a problem, and dropping it away when his reading becomes fluent. Do this practice with relatively easy material.

7. When he reads for himself for fun, have him read material written about two grade levels *below* his practice or "frustration" level. Reading for pleasure should be just that—*pleasure.*

8. Keep practice sessions short, interesting, and free from stress. If you spend too long with material in which the child needs constant help, he will turn off to reading entirely.

9. Look for phonetic clues to help your child see similarities in words. Short exercises such as finding all the words on a magazine or newspaper page which contain *ea* that says "ee," such as "each" or "reach," then having him go back and read just those words, will help him become aware of word sounds.

10. When you read and when you talk, you blend consonants into vowels. Try dividing words into syllables with this rule in mind and see how easy it is to blend syllables into words. If it seems hard for the child, print a list of words of different lengths, and let the child copy these words, using two colors or pens, such as red and blue—alternating the colors so that the syllables stand out. (It helps if you do several sample words this way. It also helps the child to have to think about how to divide the word before writing it.)

11. Another helpful technique is for you to alternate with your child in reading just syllables on lists of multi-syllable words. That is, you read one, then he reads one. Read such material long enough so that the child is programmed into reading by syllables. Then let him do syllable reading on his own. When

it becomes an automatic pattern let him *smooth it out,* running
the syllables together so that it sounds more like straight reading.
Repetitions and hesitations mean he needs to do more syllable
work at that level. Finally, use this reading by syllables technique
for harder words only. Make sure the reading is smooth, even,
and at a normal pace. Emphasize to your child that *fast reading
is not necessarily good reading, and good reading does not necessarily mean fast reading.*

Problem #8: Spelling and Phonics

*"Spelling is very difficult for my youngster. There is no way
he can memorize every word. How can I help him?"*
Probably the basis for all good spelling is a solid phonics base.
Although the English language is not entirely consistent phonetically, it follows the rules well enough to make it worthwhile to
master the principles. Dictation of phonetically spelled words
(like *information, depend*), making word families (*hook, book,
cook*), and learning some obvious exceptions should be a part
of the spelling program.
One of the most important aids for spelling is a personal spelling
list. A small notebook should be kept by each student. As much
as possible, spelling should be relevant to the subjects being studied. Words missed during the day should be copied correctly
in the notebook, then studied and vowel patterns noted. When
five to ten words have accumulated in the book, they should
be dictated to the child as a little quiz. Periodically, these words
should be reviewed with the parent or an older sibling.
When regular lists of words are studied, take time to help
the child see the structure of each word. Have him say the word
slowly, pointing to each sound as he says that sound. See if he
can write the word correctly immediately after that. Keep his
vocabulary on the stretch. If you are using the Moore-McGuffey
Readers with their excellent word lists, be sure your student
looks up in the dictionary all the words in the word lists at the
end of each chapter. Remember to make the dictionary important
to all reading, both for spelling and pronunciation.

13. Homework That Really Counts: Chores, Service, and Industry

WHEN MY BROTHER and I were seven and eight years old, Dad started us as helpers on his jobs after school and on weekends and vacations. He was a cement contractor, and we had to carry boards and heavy steel stakes. Before long, we learned to shovel sand and rock into concrete mixers. Later he gradually introduced us to wheelbarrows, at first with light loads and then heavier ones, until by age fifteen or sixteen we were proudly doing men's work. And as we accepted responsibility, he gave us more trust and more authority. I remember that by the time I was twelve I could run a mixer and by sixteen I was supervising a gang of men on a paving job. This time spent with Dad—although sometimes onerous for a lazy boy—was one of his greatest gifts to me. This was real homework, the kind that most boys need but few receive. They are too busy with self-centered sports or other amusements and assignments from school that make less sense than teaching a frog to swim.

Perhaps the second most extravagant and damaging myth in American education is the tall tale about homework. (The most dangerous myth is that children must be around many other youngsters to become "socialized," a claim we debunk elsewhere in this book.) As we write these lines, there is a powerful movement sweeping the nation that makes astonishing claims for rote homework, and parents are among the worst offenders. In all likelihood, there is not a single replicable research study that will support their claims. On the other hand, the evidence suggests that supervised study in the classroom is significantly superior to homework as commonly conceived.

True homework is work at home—chores and industries done with parents. Such manual homework provides your child with badly needed balance for a tired young brain, and there should be at least as much of this work as study. Experiments in many states from coast to coast as well as overseas have proven that "working" students at all levels perform higher scholastically than those who "study all day."

Rote homework, on the other hand, encourages dishonesty, laziness, and division in the home. Children often bring to school work that was done by their parents, or they insist on freedom from family chores in order to do their homework. Thus, in many homes, this practice creates irritation, irresponsibility and oftentimes division between parents and child, whereas children would be much better off with "talk time" as they work or sit with Mother and Dad.[1]

Work is a blessing that has come to be viewed by modern youngsters as a curse. Productive manual *work*, when done with parents and when combined with voluntary *service* at home or for neighbors or others, becomes a great healer. This combination builds self-worth as the child feels needed and depended upon. And it is probably the greatest healer for "burnout" and the surest therapy for the social cancer of peer dependency.

Work and service build initiative, industry, integrity, order, dependability, and a hundred other qualities not learned so well from books. Frugality is more easily taught when your child has his money invested in the family business, *his* business. He also learns the equality of man—all colors and economic levels—when he develops self-worth and no longer has a need to assert himself negatively.

How do you teach the nobility of work? Some mothers tell us that because they did not start early enough to teach their children to work, it is difficult to get them to work at all, to say nothing of doing it cheerfully. This is a real challenge to your ingenuity. In the first place, during the first eight to twelve years, a "let's do it together" job almost always works better than assigned chores. Suggest: "You help me clean my room [or make my bed] and I'll help you with yours." Or Daddy might say, "After you help Mother with the dishes, I'll help you fix the pedal on your bicycle." Children need things done *for* them constantly, so be sure it's a two-way affair. One of the best ways is to form a family corporation, electing officers and delegating duties.

Teach your children to concentrate on helping others more than themselves. We recall that our mothers used excellent psychology to make good workers out of us. They used to tell us how good we were at cleaning out cupboards and closets! This may not have been their favorite job, but it became ours—because we couldn't resist hearing their appreciation when we cleaned and neatly arranged the drawers and cupboards in the house and garage. Our mothers did the same with other jobs, and we responded with our very best performances. In order to be sure we wouldn't miss the corners when cleaning, they reminded us that our little fingers could get into the corner and clean better than theirs. In due time, we were brought into active participation in the family businesses or farms.

The following list includes more than two hundred kinds of work that home-schooling families are doing currently, most of which bring in a significant income. There are many books on cottage industries available from your local library, published by *Family Circle, Good Housekeeping,* and others.

Loving mothers and fathers who understand children always, somehow, find a way.

Successful Ideas for Work Programs at School or Home

Agriculture

Greenhouse	Spring Vegetable Plants
Seedlings	Shrubs and Nursery Stock
Beddable Plants	Sod Farm (Lawn Grass)

House Plants
Bees
Eggs
Lawn Care
Landscaping
Install Drip Irrigation System
Christmas Tree Farm

Vegetable Gardening
Animals: Breed, Board, Sell
Fruit Gardening (Melons, Berries,
   etc.)
Orchards
Herbs, Mushrooms, Wild Herbs

Health and Individual Care

Elderly and Convalescent Care
Retarded Children and Adults

Health Conditioning
Foster Home

Small Manufacturing and Repair

Apron Making
Wood Toys
Bee-Shipping Containers
Card Holders
Firewood
Rubber Stamps
Bookbinding
Window Boxes; Grow Boxes for
   Plants
Scratch Pads
Rope Making
Rug Weaving
Neckties and Scarves
Quilt Making
Making Fruit Dryers
Picture Frames
Garden Carts
Making and Repairing Window
   Screens
Horse-Trailer Mats
Broom and Brush Making
Ring and Buckle Making
Strap Work, Halters
Small Motors
Ski Ropes
Embroidered Shirts and Blouses
Camper Seats
Dog Harness and Collars

Making Computer ROMs
Canvas Work
Cinch Covers and Chafes
Peeling Posts and Poles
Split Shakes and Shingles
Wooden Toys and Painting
Fishing Flies
Sandals
Rifle Slings
Door Mats
Cane Seated Chairs
Metal Gates
Horse Covers
Spinning Mohair
Clothing and Shirts
Holsters
Leather Vests
Mohair and Nylon Reins (braided)
Bull Ropes
King Blankets
Hay Aprons
Trophy Buckles
Mittens and Gloves
Hat Making
Miniature Room Furniture
Plaques: Wood and Plaster
Dolls: Making, Dressing, Collecting
Auto Body Repair

Crafts

Silkscreen Printing
Badges/Cards
Shellcraft
Custom Posters—Varigraph
Leather Articles

Custom Christmas Cards
Sewing Projects: Dressmaking, Ties,
   Slipcovers, Alterations, Draperies,
   etc.
Greeting Card Illustration and Verses

Glass Specialties: Painting, Selling, etc.
Illustrating
Macrame, Wall Hangings
Mobiles
Pottery
Nature Craft (Shadow Boxes)
Belts, Billfolds, Purses
Knitting Sweaters

Basket Making
Rag Rug Braiding
Candle Making
Calligraphy
Glass Blowing
Paintings
Lamp Making
Puppet Making

Volunteer Services (*a few of many*)

Visiting Pediatric Wards
Candy-Stripers
Visiting Nursing Homes
Helping the Handicapped
Free Baby-Sitting
Baking for Church Sale

Painting Fences
Weeding Gardens
Cleaning Houses
Walking the Feeble or Elderly
Taking Wild Flowers to Aged or Ill
Rummage Sale for Needy

Merchandising

Firewood Business
Food and Garden Sales
Books, Educational Games, Educational Tools and Toys (For more information on such sales,

send a self-addressed, stamped envelope to Hewitt-Moore Publishing, Box 9, Washougal, WA 98671.)

Foods

Health Food Manufacture, Sprouts
Health Food Restaurant or Take Out
School Natural Food Store
Package and Sell Dried Fruit
Baking: Bread, Cookies, etc.
Frozen Foods
Recipe Testing
Crackerjacks
Making Sandwiches for Offices
Cooking Demonstrations
Pickle Making

Grain Sales (Rare Varieties)
School Lunches (Bagels)
Catering
Candymaking
Jellies; Jams
Soup Kitchen
Fruit Cakes
Selling Lemonade
Making Custom Vitamin Dog Biscuits

Paid Services

Typing
Yard Work
Chores at School
Bicycle Repair
Shoe Repair
Electric Appliance Repair
Packaging (Fish hooks, etc.)
Janitor Service
Cleaning Boxcars

Stuffing Envelopes
Tutoring
Child Care
Gift Wrapping
Bookkeeping
Painting Street Numbers on Curbs
Rototilling
Music, Language, or Art Lessons
Computers

Designing: Dresses, Interiors
Chores in Home
Garage Sales
Mobile-Home Repair
Shoe Polishing
Car-Wash Detail
Brake Drum Turning
Pet Grooming, Training, Boarding
House Sitting

Furniture Moving
Professional Body Massage
Painting: Furniture, Interiors
Games for Parties
House or Apartment Cleaning
Carpet Cleaning
Cooking Classes
Financial Counseling; Taxes

Construction

Buying and Fixing Up Old Houses
Cattle Guards and Chutes
Mobile Home Porch and Railing

Renovate Old Motor Homes
Horse Feeders
Building Fences

Miscellaneous

Newspaper Drives
Rubber Fence (from Tires)
Dry Cleaning and Laundry
Sanding Furniture
Taxidermy
Copy Tape Recordings
Computer Programming
Gift, Yarn or Fabric Shops
Interviewing
Magazine Subscriptions
Mail-Order Selling
Multi-level Sales Manufacturer's
    Representative
Flower Arrangements; Dried Flowers
Framing Pictures and Mirrors
Kitchen Planning
Paint Mixing
Party Favors and Decorations
Party Menus
Pattern Maker/Tester
Photography
Public Speaking
Translating
Telephone Answering Service

Stencil Making
Aluminum Cans and Bottle Returns
Printing
Coupon Clipping
Upholstery
Painting China
Antiques: Sale, Repair, Refinishing
Architecture
Employment Agency
Exercise Classes
Fashion Boutique
Packaging
Restoring Paintings
Wigs, dressed and sold
Window Shades
Writing for Advertising, Speeches,
    Publicity
Rocks and Minerals for Decorations
Public Relations
Travel Agency
Swimming Instructor
Stenographic Services
Secondhand Clothing Sales

III. Backgrounds for Great Teaching

14. What We Mean by "Curriculum"

ONCE UPON A time, Dr. G. H. Reavis, a veteran educator who was wise in the ways of curricula and who also happened to be a superintendent of the Cincinnati city schools, gave his imagination free rein. He was concerned that "progressive education," an invention of John Dewey, had begun to turn American schools from their old, simple, but stable and productive course into random thrusts at innovation—change for change's sake, rather than truly creative education. There may possibly have been some advantages to Dr. Dewey's new education, but if there were any, most teachers did not understand them. They simply renewed their efforts to put all children through the same grind regardless of their individual differences. Not surprisingly, confusion reigned, and Dr. Reavis couldn't resist describing it in terms of dumb animals. He called it "The Animal School" and conjectured that the birds and beasts wanted to do "something heroic" in education. We adapt the story here.

We assume that the schoolteacher was an ostrich, for, of all lower creatures, only ostriches treat their young as carelessly as human beings do. The teacher decided on a curriculum consisting of running, climbing, swimming, and flying. He apparently did not believe in readiness or that students are different from each other. The ostrich wanted all the animals to have approximately the same courses—much as Dr. Mortimer Adler of the

Encyclopaedia Britannica and the National Education Association advocate for all children.[1]

So-o-o, the duck got *A*'s in swimming and in flying, yet received only a *C* in tree climbing and had to stay after school because he got to the top his own way. He failed running, even though he dropped swimming to have more time for the track, and his webbed feet became tattered in his effort to excel.

The rabbit, on the other hand, went to the top of the class in running. But he finally had a nervous breakdown because of so much make-up work in swimming, and he completely failed tree climbing and flying.

The squirrel got a *D* in flying because he insisted on starting down from the top instead of taking off from the ground up. Because he developed charleyhorses from trying to run instead of hop, he even got a *C* in climbing class, where he could normally expect to excel.

Likewise, the eagle refused to climb the trees with her claws— so the ostrich gave her a *D*, even though she was the fastest of all to the top. Besides, she was severely disciplined, even though she was a girl and was generally considered to be more mature than the boys of her age.

Finally, there was an unusual tree frog who could swim exceedingly well and made a nominal attempt at running, climbing, and flying. He went to the head of the class.

The obvious lesson in this story is that it did not occur to the dumb ostrich that he might make the best of each creature's unique talents—the very purpose of all great curricula. Yet the best-publicized of recent curriculum recommendations has much of this very absurdity. Since 1976, the National Education Association (NEA) has endorsed school entry for all children at age three or four, ready or not.

The Ingredients of a Sound Curriculum

Essentially, curriculum is what you teach. It may be organized or unorganized, profitable or unprofitable, and it may lead to academic excellence or to chaos. To a large extent this depends upon you. Don't be afraid. Keep it simple—suited to your children's needs.

A common mistake made by some educators is to think of the curriculum only in terms of the basic skills, liberal arts and sciences, and similar so-called academic studies. But this is like trying to bake a loaf of well-risen bread without yeast. Perhaps the most important ingredients of our curriculum should be those factors which make up sound character—integrity, dependability, industry, initiative, order, and concern for others more than self. Of what use is a student brilliant in the sciences or a genius in mathematics or a master of oils or a person skilled in business if he is not honest and has not learned to practice the Golden Rule? This comprehensive admonition should be the underpinning for all curricula: "Do to others what you would have them do to you" (Matt. 7:12, NIV). In fact, this teaching is the one golden thread that runs through all major religions from Christianity to Confucianism and from Islam to Taoism.

First of all, we want to be sure that our curriculum has a balance which includes not only academics and their basic skills, but also manual excellence with an understanding of the work ethic, a respect for all men, and reverence for God.

Dr. Florence Stratemeyer of Columbia University, at the time considered to be the nation's leading curriculum authority, once accepted my invitation to lecture to one of my classes in an Eastern university. After looking over the outline of our course and fingering several of the books we were using, she said, "If you follow your philosophy of education as outlined here, you must teach a child to know *why* he acts. He must learn how to think, how to reason, for himself." She underscored these objectives as great goals in the development of curricula. Then she added, quoting in part, from our course of study:

> The education that consists in the training of the memory only and which tends to discourage self direction and independent thought has a moral bearing which is too little appreciated. The student tends to look to his peers instead of to sound behavioral standards. As this student sacrifices the power to reason and to judge for himself,

he becomes incapable of discriminating between truth and error, and falls easy prey to deception. It is a fact widely ignored, though never without danger, that error rarely appears for what it really is.

It is crucial in the development of the curriculum that both the teacher and the student have some idea of why each is doing what he is doing. There must be some absolutes, lest the teacher and student be like waves which are driven and tossed by the wind. Most of us are easily led to follow tradition and customs. We adults, too, have become afflicted with the social cancer of peer dependency. Our *philosophy*—our idea of truth and whether it is relative or absolute—will be the father of our curriculum which our *goals* help develop. After that will come an appraisal of the *resources* available. And finally there are the *methods* we devise to utilize those resources—in order to reach the goals based upon our philosophy.

Beyond the Three R's

Thus, we are concerned in educating the whole learner—mentally, physically, spiritually, and socially. The 4-H clubs call this "head, hand, heart, health." Tradition, custom, and conventional wisdom and practice must surrender to moral absolutes or society cannot survive. The curriculum must go well beyond the Three R's, the *ABCD*'s, and the normal requirements for health and safety; it must center on the character education of the child. When this takes place, all the conventional items that are necessary will follow along in their wake.

We emphasize that while the curriculum does include book learning, it must go far beyond that to provide for character development. For this, books are generally less important than practical and manual work, and service to others in the home, community and nation. No curriculum builds self-worth without this balance, nor does it bring fulfillment so complete.

15. The Psychologists Call It "Cognition"—But They Really Mean Consistent Reasoning

WHEN I WAS a five-year-old in the San Pablo, California, public schools, I remember worrying about Humpty Dumpty, the "egg" supposedly broken to bits in his fall from the wall. Then I felt better when I realized that he was put together again. It didn't occur to me that this was all silly talk until a year or so later when *I* tried to put an egg together. We also read stories about how the moon was made of green cheese. The fact that I wondered a bit about the green color was a suggestion that my reasoning was approaching maturity, for I was relating the moon to the white or orange color of most cheeses I knew. I was becoming "cognitively mature."

Both the quality and maturity of a child's socialization on the one hand, and his ability to do thoughtful learning on the other, depend largely on his *cognitive ability*—the extent to which he can *consistently reason* from cause to effect or understand the basic *whys* and *hows* of living. This in turn depends also on the breadth of his information, which is so dependent upon freedom to explore in the early years. Cognition is commonly discussed but seldom understood or considered beyond the concept of basic learning.

Cognition is particularly crucial for *positive socialization*. The child who is sent to kindergarten or first grade with groups of his peers, say at age five, will in all probability be negatively influenced by their manners, habits, speech, dress, rivalry, and ridicule. Professor Urie Bronfenbrenner of Cornell University calls this "social contagion." [1] And Stanford studies by Albert Bandura and by others confirm our fears that this is pervasive even at the preschool level.[2] When a child comes home from school and shocks you with undesirable new words or finger signs, you try to explain carefully how "nasty" they are. Since he is not yet able to reason consistently, he may not understand your explanations about *why* they are nasty, but instead will turn from your values and follow his peers because "everybody's doing it." He simply is not cognitively ready for your explanation.

Psychologists talk about "cognition," but they might just as well at times call it *good judgment* or *common sense* or *discrimination* or simply learning to make sound choices and becoming thoughtful. Whatever term is used, a child's breadth of experience is vitally important—a dimension usually enhanced far more by freedom at home than by the restrictions of the classroom and school bus.

Thoughtfulness on behalf of others is not only an ideal to be cherished, but it is the bottom line in learning. If your student does not know the *why* of his math problem, he may neither long remember it nor apply it. Typical rote learning dries up the young mind. I had a college trigonometry professor who mutilated our love for math simply by assuming that we students understood the *principles,* for example, of the sine and the cosine and the operation of the slide rule. He was a fine old man, but a loss as a teacher. He not only knew his subject "too well," but he was too thoughtless to really share it. At age eighty-five, he was reversing the cognitive process and becoming like a child.

The fruits of cognitive maturity are to be cherished. If young trees are treated carelessly, they may be stunted; but if they are cultivated carefully—pruned tenderly and given room to grow, and not left to the random contagions waiting at every hand— the chances are that they will grow to full and beautiful maturity. Just so, the child who is carefully and lovingly nurtured will grow in stature and wisdom and in favor with both God and man.

16. How Children Develop

A FEW YEARS ago, several of us were talking to a large audience at the annual meeting of the National Association for the Education of Young Children (NAEYC) at the Atlanta Civic Auditorium. The chairwoman, an elderly and eminent early-schooling specialist, had told me the night before, "I really like you, Dr. Moore, but I am going to do everything I can to prove you wrong." And she tried her best—manipulating time, questions, and emphases in general—as I called early schooling to account.

Encouraged by the chairwoman's effort, a Harvard-educated lawyer, one of America's "ten outstanding women," stood up after my talk on early-childhood research. "To hell with research," she shouted, "let's have action." Captivated by her charisma, the audience roared its approval. Yet she was the head of the Children's Defense Fund.

When it was my turn again, I asked them if they thought it was reasonable for them to ask for research on tires, airplanes, drugs, and other "necessities"—and yet be indifferent about research on children. The crowd saw the point, reversed its field, and roared for research. Yet, in the end, manipulated in part by the chairwoman, they called for more early schooling—which is clearly shown by replicable research to be damaging for normal children in every way. (See Introduction for research-based studies on child development.)

Here was a typical case study of a Western phenomenon that applauds research in education, but has little use for findings that demand societal change. Accordingly, we find that many teacher-educators, either ignorant or discouraged, largely neglect essential research on children and learning. Few teacher-education programs provide more than a tentative introduction to understanding children's developmental needs. After all, social and political pressure and traditions are not easy to confront. The educators give the public what it wants—earlier schooling, *Sesame Street,* Little League, and a wide variety of child-wrecking exercises.

In this section we offer a short course on how children develop, in the hope that a few parents and teachers might better understand developmental stages, and thus how to meet the needs of normal children in coordination, communication, reasoning (cognition), self-help, social skills, developmental tasks, and special requirements. How children learn, react, and develop on all levels is still a relatively obscure science for most educators. Home-economics teachers, on the other hand, are usually quite thorough in this, so if you need any special help they are more likely to be able to provide you with answers.

Developmental psychology is in some respects the most important academic learning a parent or teacher can have. Teachers or parents often teach routinely, expecting their children to learn things that are entirely out of their range. Yet, perhaps just as often, these adults give their children studies that are easy for them, and don't keep their minds challenged. It must be understood that children of a given age may vary as much as three to five years in their readiness for a particular type of learning. This doesn't mean, however, that the child who is late in learning to catch a ball is necessarily dull. He may be among the brightest, but merely slow in developing that particular skill. It is also commonly verified that boys are slower than girls in cognitive development—the ability to reason consistently from cause to effect. On the other hand, little boys will often be ahead of little girls in arithmetic skills.

We urge you, therefore, as you read the following discussion, to remember what has been said here and in our earlier books about the differences between children. For example, some children may be toilet-trained at fifteen or eighteen months, while others may require thirty months or more.

Behavior Typical of Ages Three through Six

The child of three to six years old is usually a great talker, asking many questions to which we hope you will respond. You don't have to answer silly questions foolishly: in general, treat the child seriously and he (or she, of course) will learn rapidly. Keep his mind reaching. Sometimes his queries are indicative of other concerns—differences in age and maturity from his peers or between boys and girls, worries about family problems, and so on. As children grow older they will develop new kinds of fears and will also be more aware of dangers than heretofore.

As a child grows into the fifth and sixth years, you can use him to help teach younger members of the family. If he feels that they are part of his responsibility, there will be less likelihood of his displaying jealousy and aggressiveness toward them. Such constructive and positive habits and attitudes will also keep him from regressing in his patterns of eating, toilet control, and so on.

At five and six, a child is beginning to become a distinctively social creature. He does not yet reason consistently from cause to effect nor judge motives clearly, but he is trying to develop self-direction. This may result in flares of temper or exhibitions of real courage. He needs your example and your steady, encouraging hand. Socially, he does not need a lot of children as much as he needs your assurance that he is wanted and depended upon. This will build self-worth and positive sociability.

Remember, he is not a little adult, but rather still a child. Give him time to get his concepts together. What to you is "crooked," to him may be *straight*. What to you is "simple" may be very *complex* to him. What to you is "near," to him is *far*, and what to you is "young" seems *old* to a child's mind. (To a six-year-old, a twenty-year-old is "over the hill.") What to you is "small," to him is *large*. And your idea of "short" is *extended* or *long* to him. You, of course, have already found that what to you seems "messy" might be quite acceptable and orderly in his thinking. Your "dirty" is his *clean*. You may be certain that something is "impure" or "contaminated," but it will appear lovely and sterile to him. Finally, many things you think are "inappropriate" may appear to children to be quite acceptable, especially if all of their peers are doing them.

In other words, if they are to have good values, children of this age group urgently need your example, undiluted by that of their peers. On the other hand, if your values are less worthy than those of the school, it might be better to enroll him! Your three- to six-year-old prefers to play with those of his own sex, but will usually quite readily play with both boys and girls, particularly if you encourage this. There are increasing tendencies toward sociability, but don't mistake this for a need to have many encounters with peers, for the more of these he has, the fewer *meaningful* human contacts will be made. You will be wise to be on guard about a child's friends. In other words, give him the freedom of a little lamb, but remember that the shepherd always knows where his young sheep are.

Now is the time for your child to learn to cooperate—to limit aggressiveness and avoid indecency. If activities revolve around the home, they will be less likely to center on his playmates and the social contagion that is rampant "out there." Your young one has many winning ways and is hoping for admiration. Remember that activities with you, helping and working with you, are among a child's highest forms of play, especially if he sees the outcome of his work. Gardens are particularly worthwhile. He can plant the seeds, cultivate and watch the plants grow, and then harvest, and there is no greater learning experience than this. But it must be done *with you* to have maximum effect. Don't be terribly surprised if your child tends to be a little boy (or girl). A generous opportunity for constructive experiences with you will turn aggressive responses into positive, assertive behavior.

Be alert to a tendency to "play house," particularly with the opposite sex, for there is often a mutual exploration of genitals at this age. Children from three to six are not too young to learn the naughty words you would prefer were not in their vocabulary. This does not indicate an abnormal sexual interest, but rather a curiosity which needs your guidance and supervision.

As much as he is like others, remember that your child is a unique individual who needs, wants, and depends upon you, who very much cherishes *your* dependency and need for him in a warm and loving way. The three- to six-year-old finds security in routine and in perimeters that you set consistently. In other words, this is not the time for indulgence, but for stipulated and clear lines of behavior that you expect him to observe. This may require occasional punishment, even a switching at times. But if you must discipline, make sure that you do it in patience and love, carefully explaining why and following the punishment with a hug or other gesture of love. Never mistake indulgence for love, for firm kindness is what a child needs.

As children approach the latter part of this age period, they will begin to show loyalty to playmates and perhaps a devotion to other adults besides you, particularly if there are relatives or others at hand. Don't feel threatened, for this is normal. Just continue to make them feel needed, while encouraging them toward carrying responsibility. This period and the next two years will largely determine the kind of personality, character, and attitude toward the world that your child will have throughout life.

Behavior Typical of Ages Six through Eight

Bear in mind that there may be wide differences in any two given children as they mature, especially between a boy and a girl. You may have observed that some children walk at nine months, while others wait until they are twice that age. There may be startling individual differences during the six- to eight-year-old span, with children varying as much as four or five years in some kinds of maturity. This is the time when the child begins to come into his own.

Many people insist that this is also the period when he needs to be recognized by his peer group. However, we are quick to point out that if you want your child to be recognized in this way, make sure that he first has the experience of feeling needed and depended upon at home. This is what builds a sense of self-worth, not associating with a lot of other children and having to knuckle under to their values. A peer-dependent child can lose not only his sense of self-worth and optimism for the future, but also his respect for you and a trust in his peers.

Nevertheless, we do not suggest that you totally restrict association with other children. Don't put your child in a social strait-jacket. In general, if you give him tools instead of toys and carry him into service-oriented activities such as helping the needy, you will see a positive personality and character develop. Earlier dependency upon the family will move into a wholesome independence. There will also be less likelihood of his experiencing stressful situations and becoming angered, frustrated, and so on. Children at this age are normally involved in a good deal of rivalry with peers. They do not need this, as we've already noted. Rivalry does not breed nobility.

If your children can be at home with you until eight to ten or later, they will avoid the tiring and lonely experiences that school often affords—and the self-doubts that so often tear down a sense of personal worth. This is particularly true of boys, who lag behind girls in maturity and thus are at a disadvantage in both learning and behavior at school. If you begin a child's formal schooling at about eight or later and don't hold him to more than about an hour and a half of face-to-face or side-by-side teaching—and then work with him and also allow for adequate rest time—he will be less likely to exhibit the exhaustion or burn-out that is so common these days and the hyperactivity that is often seen among children who are in school. There will be much less of the defiance and anger that is created by conflicting tugs from the home and the school at this age.

Don't think that your child is unusual if he tends to disregard your parental requirements, especially in terms of manners, cleanliness, and order. He is either consciously or unconsciously testing you. If you rise to the challenge of taking him into your confidence, he'll be less likely to be aggressive or depressed—or worse, withdrawn.

This is also a time when most youngsters in this age group will be careless about personal effects, unless you have anticipated this stage and developed a system since the earlier years. It will help if your example is sound. If you give these children daily success experiences—even if you have to plan them—they will be less likely to have feelings of failure, inferiority, rejection, or isolation. Let them know that you have very specific goals in mind for them. Make a list of explicit things to do each day, and let the children check these things off and sense their dependability a-building. Never allow opportunities for evading instructions—a behavior common at this age.

Encourage positive feelings about the child's age-mates, respect for those who are older, and tenderness for those who are younger. As ever, your example will teach a great deal. Otherwise, you might expect a child to be critical and even abusive of others. Children are among the most cruel of all animals. They tend to be particularly rude to the handicapped—those who cannot defend themselves. Explain the background of such individuals, so your own children can understand how and why such things happen—from birth injuries, car accidents, or other misfortunes. This does not mean that you will discourage friendships with well-behaved and attractive children, but that you will give your child a balanced perspective.

Occasionally your child will defy you and test your mettle. Be sure you are right in your reaction! There may be times when you are wrong and may have to apologize. Don't be afraid to do this, but try to ensure that the occasions are few. Your children will respect you deeply and will build a love for you that will last a lifetime.

Behavior Typical of the Nine-Year-Old

As children approach the ninth year, they sense that they are growing out of childhood and do not want to be treated as children. They want to be respected as competent persons. But you know well that authority must always be kept commensurate with responsibility. You can safely provide only such freedom as they can handle.

As your children near nine, girls tend to move toward feminine roles and boys toward more masculine ways. Boys also tend to become more dominant and to stress skill, strength, and daring. They generally find less comfort and release in crying, sensing that this is something he is expected to put away. A girl usually senses that she must become less "boyish," less aggressive physically, and should avoid tendencies to appear masculine.

Although there may have already been some involvement, now is the time when masturbation appears among many youngsters, especially those who are not outgoing and those who have a less than desirable amount of self-worth. While this is particularly true among boys, it has been increasingly a part of girlhood, as well. Contrary to what many psychologists and even ministers are saying these days, we believe that masturbation is neither necessary nor "normal."

Pediatricians who are not influenced by such avant-garde thinking see clearly the deteriorating affects of habitual masturbation. Such children do not generally do well in their school work. There may be marked listlessness, and the children are often watery-eyed and asocial.

Help your child to understand that masturbation is not productive. The sex organs were designed for truly creative and recreative purposes, and any violation of this principle tends toward homosexuality. We are not implying that masturbators inevitably become gays, but we are suggesting that *to the extent the use of the sex organs focuses on self, the acts are not heterosexually productive, and to the extent that they violate heterosexuality, they are destructive.* To those who suggest that masturbation is impossible to overcome, we suggest that their expectancies are far too low. We have worked with literally thousands of such youngsters who have changed their focus—physically, mentally, spiritually, and socially—when they discovered the futility of their actions.

We repeat (and stress at the risk of your good will) that it is not necessary for a child to become involved in rivalry games at this age, although that is a natural tendency. Constructive activities, such as in agricultural or recreational clubs and in church groups, are excellent avenues for a natural inclination to be with peers. This is not to deny a child play, but to suggest that work *with you* is the most fulfilling activity. When children do play, try games that don't selfishly excite. For example, when playing team ball, exchange at least one player between teams each inning or quarter or other period of time. Or rotate around the net in a volleyball game.

Remember that children also tend to place their confidence in their age-mates. It is easy for children to be defensive of their peers, so be on your guard when you discuss them.

It is still important that you draw the line when your children's judgment is not sound. You can build and guide their sense of self-direction, so that their own orders to themselves will coincide with yours. This can be done, as we have noted before, by working with your children and by getting them into service activities on behalf of those older, weaker, or less fortunate.

Nine-year-olds are beginning to understand the importance of order and may be becoming quite oriented to rules. This is also the time to take advantage of their desire to do things in a right way—by helping them put things away, meet appointments on time, and avoid conflict by being thoughtful of others.

Behavior Typical of Ages Ten to Twelve

Children anywhere from nine on up to twelve will usually be quite easily persuaded to "try, try, try again." If they are at home during these years, they will sacrifice less of their creativity than if you put them in school—assuming that you have responded to them and provided a great deal of freedom to explore.

Since children of this age cannot stand failure easily, daily success experiences are important. Work experience, substituting tools for toys, is also very important at this point, especially if the work is done with their parents in the kitchen, garage, or garden. This will also help greatly in establishing the sexuality of a girl or boy.

Don't be offended if your child is now looking toward others as well as toward you for his authority figures. If he develops a strong sense of self-worth, this will not become a serious problem. Furthermore, if you have treated your children with affection and warm embraces and kisses in their earlier years, there will be less likelihood that they will now be embarrassed in public when you react warmly to them.

You may begin to see important physical changes during this period, particularly with young women, who often begin menstruation before age twelve. Don't be surprised at the moodiness that almost inevitably comes from the glandular changes marking the transition to puberty and adolescence. This may also be a confusing time for boys, who simply do not understand what girls are going through, because they are usually not as mature and never have to experience such radical physical changes.

As these youngsters move up toward eleven and twelve, they do indeed find themselves in a no-man's-land in which they are uncertain, often unappreciative of their elders, and have little use for younger brothers and sisters. If you have anticipated this and have used your child as a mentor for younger siblings, you can help him realize that with emerging authority and freedom must come certain responsibilities.

Also about this time, conscience becomes a troubling factor. This is usually less of a problem for those who have a sound sense of self-worth and who have found a steady religious experience. If a child is skillful with his hands and has become accustomed to serving those less fortunate than himself, he will be less likely to be overly concerned by self-doubts.

Remember that your child is now approaching the age of responsibility. From this time on, he should be held more and more accountable for his own behavior. While it is still important that you set guidelines and limits, remind him of the qualities that pay off—dependability, thoughtfulness, neatness and order, industry and initiative. He should now appreciate the importance of the Golden Rule and be increasingly appreciative of the meaning of real freedom and of his unique place in the world. Give your child every opportunity at this age to evaluate various trades and professions, so that he is not left to wander aimlessly as he goes into his complex adolescent years.

Understanding these first twelve years and applying this insight systematically in your home and classroom will lay an all-important foundation for your teaching and can turn a child with an unhappy and unproductive past experience into a happy young person looking ahead to a fruitful life. There is no one who can normally do this better than you, and the fewer who interfere with this process, the better.

17. Readiness and the Truth about "Super Baby"

I READ IN *Time* magazine one day in 1971 that California State School Superintendent Wilson Riles had gone on record as stating that "readiness is outmoded" in educating young children.[1] I knew that Dr. Riles was urging early schooling down to age two and one-half for all California toddlers, but I couldn't believe that he had said, in effect, that they did not have to be "ready" in order to be schooled. So I telephoned him.

"I have sometimes been misquoted by the press, including *Time*," I began, in an effort to make easier his denial of the statement. "Did you actually say that readiness is outmoded?"

"Yes," he replied, "*Time* quoted me correctly."

I soon broke off the conversation, both in pity that a man of his stature had no greater understanding of children—and in shock that he had so publicly displayed his ignorance.

The Risks of Ignoring Readiness

Imagine what would happen if you threw out the principle of readiness in the development of your infant. For example, what if you were to discard diapers when your baby began to walk at nine to fifteen months? You would be cleaning up messes all over the house. Or ignoring stairways, hot stoves, swimming pools, or medicines left randomly around? You would be taking risks every moment. That is exactly what you do if you forsake the ideal of readiness in learning. You risk anxiety, frustration, neurosis, learning failure, delinquency, loss of self-worth, and even psychosis and suicide.[2]

One Los Angeles pediatrician even extends the Riles reasoning to sex. She assumes that if the child has the sexual equipment, it should be used—for sex. So she recommends such relations among both children and adults, including incest, reasoning that you are never too young to learn about and enjoy sexual relations.

Even a beast knows better than to rush its young. Yet young mothers and fathers vie daily to enter their little ones into institutions or programs that are every bit as ridiculous—and in many respects as damaging.

Some dear friends visited us not long ago with exciting news. They had just made their first payment on a course that would "make geniuses" out of children by teaching them their basic skills by two or three. They had joined an impressive-sounding "national academy." We do not ridicule these parents, yet we do have feelings of pity for their children. They are set on a course which almost always brings more damage than gain.

Packaging "Super Baby"

Magazines are full of news of "super baby." We learn about parents, including some home-schoolers, who are fascinated by the literature and seminars which urge acceleration of learning and development in young children. We have also seen wide promotional schemes to "teach your baby to read," with large flash cards to build a reading vocabulary at a very early age. What is the use of such a parental ego-exercise for a child who is not yet able to reason enough to discover meaning in the program? It is true that, as soon as a child can repeat numbers, he can memorize the multiplication tables—but what good will this do him, when he can't possibly understand the meaning of what multiplying involves and also has no place to apply it? This is like giving him a course in steam-shovel operation and only a backyard sandpile for an excavation area. Expending energy on memorizing multiplication facts, he is distracted from far more important basic learning.

Such a child generally misses the best learning of all: through free exploration and experimentation, discovering how ordinary things in life work. For instance, as he plays with various containers and water in the tub, sink, or outdoor play pool, he can learn that some things float and some sink, that it takes more to fill a large container than a small one, that water runs through a sieve or a hole, and that a sponge or towel absorb water. He misses many of the thousands of pegs on which he can hang other information—colors, textures, smells, birds, bees, leaves, flowers, bugs, and all of nature's revelations. Arnold Gesell, the great Yale child specialist, said that if you really want a superior child, you should just take him out into nature and be quiet while nature does the teaching.[3] This is the proven way to make "super babies," as research, experience, and common sense testify.

A child we once knew could recognize and name all the presidents of the United States at age three. His parents reveled in his "genius." But what good was that information if he had no understanding of what a president is? (Incidentally, he was no whiz as an adult.) Many children are ready to recite the alphabet by age two or three—and there is no real harm in such learning. But it builds no particular genius, since they really have little use for the alphabet. High-quality reading is more than the rote memory of words taught by early flash-card drills. If, instead of depending on memory alone, the parent is willing to delay formal learning until reason and understanding have begun to mature—usually around eight to ten—the child can build a logical network of phonetic elements and word families and multiply his vocabulary rapidly. By then, of course, he will have developed, through your encouragement and responsiveness, a background of practical experiences and general knowledge that will make his reading truly meaningful and exciting. Then there is no need to struggle through tedious drill, repetition, or even unstimulating pre-primers.

Usually these naturally ready children are reading far ahead of their peers after a few months of instruction. And they have done this without the risk of burnout, anxiety, frustration, dyslexia, and neurosis, which many of these rushed children experience. They pay a high price for their parents' ignorance, ego, and folly.

Baby academies and institutes are usually like old-fashioned patent medicines, which raise parental hopes that cannot possibly be justified by research or practice. To our knowledge, such programs are not supported by a single reputable research organization or any replicable studies relating to the total development of the child. We have done extensive research analyses on early education and believe these organizations should offer evidence of their programs' soundness before they take your money. Their tactics remind us of the old practice of giving the patient mercury for an internal infection which only poisoned him more. Baby academies take from your child the right and privilege of natural, unpressured development.

Some programs have centered on children who were severely handicapped or who had been brain damaged at birth or in accidents. Professionals sometimes do marvelous things with such children, whom we agree must often be treated differently from normal youngsters. Yet all such programs must be thoroughly scrutinized before being embraced.

In the *Archives of Physical Medicine and Rehabilitation,* (vol. 49, no. 4, April 1968), an official statement was made by seven prestigious scientific groups which discredits the two most prominent such programs for infants and many of their claims of cures, which include making normal children superior, easing world tensions, and "hastening the evolutionary process." These organizations include: American Academy for Cerebral Palsy, American Academy of Physical Medicine and Rehabilitation, American Congress of Rehabilitation Medicine, Canadian Association for Children with Learning Disabilities, Canadian Association for Retarded Citizens, Canadian Rehabilitation Council for the Disabled, National Association for Retarded Children. They summarize the Doman theories thus:

> There is no empirical evidence to substantiate the value of either the theory or practice of neurological organization [i.e., "organizing the infant mind to perform advanced mental feats"]. . . . If the theory

is to be taken seriously . . . its advocates are under an obligation to provide reasonable support for the tenets of the theory and a series of experimental investigations, consistent with scientific standards which test the efficacy of the rationale.

Another claim was that reading problems could be *cured* with some of the same methods. And still later they offered "stimulation therapy" for infants to gain high levels of coordination and intelligence. A human development specialist from Salt Lake City sent us a weird advertisement he had clipped in which these neurological organizers suggested that "nurseries should be more like discos." He appended this comment: "This technique with all its noise and flashes, would appear to damage normal reflexive mental reactions and potentially cause hyperactivity and damage to the extent that nothing short of flashing lights would hold a child's short attention span for any length of time." Parents who supply or permit video games should take a lesson!

Developmental Balance

You may have noticed in your child (or other young children) that when making particular progress in one area—learning to walk, let's say—he may temporarily hit a plateau or even regress in speech or other development. The same principle holds true if there is an overemphasis on academic learning. Some other growth is hindered. A balanced development is our goal—a reasonable, logical progression to various stages of readiness. A child should talk and reason before reading, understand math concepts before doing formal number work, and develop muscular coordination before writing.

Of course, large-print books and fun learning games without pressure at home are far less damaging than a school routine, but their use is much like building the superstructure of a building before laying a firm foundation. We find that most children learn to read quite naturally—if they have been read to consistently, if their questions have been answered, and if their parents have been alert to their needs and take advantage of the teachable moments. Yet many children are simply not ready to read until age eight, and some cannot read until ten or later, even though they may be bright.

It is more important to help your child learn about everything in the world *as* it is, before he *reads* about the world. Be less concerned about your children's reading than about their developing a wide acquaintance with their environment. The problem is that many parents allow their children to grow up "untaught" generally—without responsibilities and with little real training or practical knowledge. We do not endorse such carelessness. We believe that parents are their children's very best teachers and have a responsibility to help them "increase in wisdom and stature and in favor with God and man." This includes mental, physical, spiritual, and social development. The best early curriculum includes true, inspirational and constructive stories; nature study; useful work; service; and broad life experiences.

Educational sharks are ever waiting to take advantage of the poor little fishes who are not on guard. They urge early formal music, ballet, and gymnastics—where parental ego is more on the line than the readiness of the child. Ask the "super baby" theorists and other early-formal-schooling proponents for their evidence, and make sure that you check it out thoroughly. Such merchandisers may shout loudly and take your money, but their claims cannot be substantiated by clear-cut examples of individuals who have arrived at maturity without damage. All the laws of child development and learning are against them. And, as we have noted, you have reason to fear the consequences. There is a heavy price to pay for indulging parental egos at the expense of child development.

IV. Some Things to Make Your Life Easier

18. Your Child's Best Socializer

AT A RECENT outing of home-schooling families, nearby campers commented on the behavior of the children—their initiative and industrious ways, their free mingling with adults, and their genuine interest in adult activities and conversation. "Most kids," noted an attorney, "keep pretty much to themselves or with youngsters their own ages, but I don't see that here." The lawyer was a keen observer, for children who have been home-schooled from their early years are seldom age-segregated. They mix freely with all ages, and their curiosity and exploration are accordingly larger and wider.

Most people these days tend to regard socialization as a random mixing of people, without serious thought about the quality of the mixture. In school, socialization is usually thought of in connection with a given age-grade group. The truth is that sociability is either positive or negative; it is never neutral. *Positive sociability* is the sum of mutual trust, cooperation, kindness, social responsibility, and altruism—best expressed by the Golden Rule's concern for others. *Negative sociability* involves ridicule, rivalry, antagonism, alienation, and narcissism—the "me-first" attitude so prevalent today in homes, schools, business and sports.

Strangely enough, most parents and teachers are certain that little children need to be around many other youngsters in order to be "socialized." This is perhaps the most dangerous and extravagant myth in education and child rearing today. Parents will even concede that academics might be handled at home, but will still insist that young people need a lot of group association in order to learn to get along with other children. Most adults believe that school provides the answer to youngsters' social needs. Neither the conclusions of sound research nor the voice of common sense give even a penny's worth of credibility to this convenient notion.

By its very nature school is not set up for such sensitive training. In the first place, children do not respond well to large groups. They become nervous, overexcited, and disoriented by confusion, noise, and too many people. Research clearly verifies that the more people there are around your children, the less opportunity they have for meaningful social contact. Most children relate to only about as many people as they are years old, and not necessarily for long periods of time. Psychologists have found, as many parents know instinctively that peaceful solitude is necessary for mental health and that the less cluttered your children's routine, the more secure they will be.

In the typical school, children cannot be treated with any partiality—individually or personally—but only as an integral part of the class. In spite of the fact that children of the same age vary greatly in ability, achievement, background, and personality, they must more or less go through the same assembly line— doing the same thing at the same time and fitting roughly into the same mold as the others. In truth, the partiality needed by the young child brings the feeling that he is special to his parents— loved and cherished as a unique individual. These forced omissions and most schools' overwhelming concern for subject matter greatly interfere with free exploration and the child's development as a unique person.

Contrast the school routine with the opportunities your youngster has in a reasonably well-regulated, loving home. Here he experiences relative quiet and simplicity in his daily program; one-to-one responses to his questions, needs, and interest, practically on call; and the opportunity for solitude. As he is allowed to associate closely with his parents in their daily activities of work, play, rest, and conversation, the child shares responsibility and feels that he is part of the family team—needed, wanted, and depended upon. And thereby he develops a sense of self-worth, the cornerstone of positive socialization.

When he does enter school, preferably not before eight or ten or even twelve, he usually becomes a social leader because he is already confident and independent in his thinking and in his values. He largely avoids the temptation to follow the crowd and becomes the productive, self-directed, and potentially excellent citizen this country so badly needs.

Good social values are not transmitted through the genes. Rather, young children learn by observation and imitation. What they see and hear makes an indelible impression on their minds and thus their actions and habits, which are difficult to erase entirely. What youngsters need most of all are good models to copy: adults, especially parents, who exemplify the kind of values they should acquire and who are concerned enough to help them develop these qualities. They will adopt the behavior, attitudes, language, and even the tone of voice of the older members of the family. Children's goals and ideals are also pretty well set by the behavior of the parents—but only if they have not already been separated from them by peer dependence.

We are convinced that if children do not have a close and almost continuous identification with their parents in these most impressionable early years, they will become indifferent to family values—even reject them—and latch onto their peers.

Because of the exposure of many very young children to early out-of-home care, the shift from parental to peer dependence may be well developed by the preschool level. A generation ago, this was noticeable only among teenagers. Unfortunately, since their young peers are generally not carriers of sound ethical values, the children learn bad habits and manners, but not the difference of right from wrong, the reason for rules, or the value of work. As we have emphasized, until the age range of about eight to twelve, children are not consistently reasonable.

Some might call this "social contagion," because it spreads through the group like a disease. A better name is "social cancer," for it is that hard to cure. At least up to the sixth grade, according to Cornell University studies, children who spend less of their elective time with their parents than with their peers tend to become peer-dependent. This robs them of self-worth, optimism and self-direction, respect for their parents and others, and even trust in their peers. What do they have left? Here you see the roots of the rebel culture of the 1960s and the drug and free sex ethics of the current generation.

The results of recent University of North Carolina day-care studies give a tragic picture of the negative socialization that takes place in an environment consisting of groups of young children with too few adults.[1] These children were found to be involved in fifteen times more acts of negative aggression than children cared for in the home. This did not represent greater assertiveness or willingness to stand up for their rights, but rather a tendency toward physical and verbal attacks on others. The children were not only more active, but also more easily frustrated, less cooperative, more distractible, less task-oriented, more egocentric, more child-oriented than adult-oriented, and more demanding of immediate gratification.

The trend toward separating little children from their parents at earlier and earlier ages—and substituting the age-segregated peer group as the source of social values—is a deceitfully dangerous form of child abuse, for it robs the child of his own identity and melds him into the crowd. He senses rejection—which can be worse than a beating. These naïve children like to be only with their peers, sacrificing the remarkable benefits of wider association. This situation promises such ominous results as violence, alienation, narcissism, and other antisocial and amoral qualities rampant in our society. Home-schooled children, on the other hand, are usually comfortable with social groups of all ages, and able to converse meaningfully with them.

To summarize, we believe that, wherever possible, home is by far the best nest until *at least* eight, ten, or twelve. Psychologists and psychiatrists who understand child development would prefer an even later age. In a reasonably warm home, parent-child responses, the true *ABC*'s of sound education, are likely to be a hundred times more frequent than the average teacher-child responses in a classroom. Where there is any reasonable doubt about the influence of schools on our children (morality, ridicule, rivalry, denial of religious values), home schools are usually a highly desirable alternative. Some thirty-five states permit them by law under various conditions. Other states rule more by policy than by law, and yet others permit home schools through court decisions.

Positive socialization is also better developed in a program where study is balanced with practical work and service. This helps to mix the sexes in a natural way, bringing boy and girl together in a wholesome, constructive camaraderie that is not available in a program centered on amusements and sports. Such a balanced approach also brings about deeper and broader understanding of others and their problems. Even racial tensions are eased.

If we are to believe sociologists J. D. Unwin [2] or Carle Zimmerman,[3] we must spend more time at home with our children in constructive work and service, lest our society be lost as were Greece and Rome. Our society's conditions are now virtually identical to theirs. Let's have more loving firmness, less indulgence toward our children. They need more work with you, the parents; fewer toys; more service for others; less sports and amusements (which tend to put self ahead of others); more self-control, patriotism, productiveness, and responsibility—in short, they need guidance along the path to self-worth as children of God. Parents and home, undiluted, usually do these things best.[4]

19. A Place for Grandparents, Too *

WHEN DORCAS MOORE died and left two little boys and a tiny daughter in the sole custody of Charles Moore, the grief-stricken widower quickly sent for his mother, our Grandmother Moore, herself long bereaved. Grandma stepped on board like an experienced railroad conductor. She had her signals straight: she could tell red from green and she knew when to pull the whistle, when to gently brake, and when to go full steam ahead. She knew Dad, his values, his "kiddies," and his home. And she stayed on the track, setting a comfortable, straight, loving course for us for five years until Dad remarried. Here was grandparenting at its best—by a strong person with values like her son's, who had clear goals and was fully appreciated by us all.

This was over sixty years ago. All is not so smooth as we near the end of the twentieth century—these days of family dispersal and fractured values, when children are taught in school to claim their "rights" and not worry so much about the old folks

* Parts of this chapter are adapted by the authors from a paper presented at Homerton College, Cambridge, England on October 13, 1982 by Dr. Robert Strom and Shirley Strom of the Office of Parent Development International at Arizona State University, Tempe, AZ 85287 (in which the authors are research associates) and published in the Cambridge Journal of Education, vol. 13, no. 1, 1983, pp. 25–28. (Used with permission.)

(nor be so respectful of them). So many grandmothers and grand-fathers feel that they are no longer needed, when, in fact, their experience and care are one of our greatest resources today.

We often receive letters from parents asking about using grand-parents in home schools. This is great when grandparents have sound values and are easy to get along with. There are also letters from grandparents who are deeply interested in their children's teaching their grandchildren at home. We like this, too. Those families that make the greatest contribution to their society are those that work together at all levels.

We have often pointed out that those parents who institutional-ize their children early will themselves be institutionalized early. Many senior citizens are experiencing this very phenomenon to-day. As they grow older, this can be one of the great fears which can destroy otherwise productive lives—that they will be dis-carded as they age and are no longer needed in the family. The attitude of many young parents is that their parents are pretty much "over the hill" and have lost their creativity. We would like to alter this view, and we believe that well-informed, home-schooling parents can help make the difference.

Teaching by Storytelling

Grandma Moore was a great storyteller! We learned much history from her, including some of our own roots. Fortunately, long-term memory does not decline significantly as we grow older, and grandparents have always been a primary source of informa-tion about events and emotions of many years before. Grandpar-ents seem to have an unlimited supply of stories to tell, and their personality and individual style gives life and charm no matter what the story content. But like all historians, grandpar-ents share responsibility to identify the experiences which most deserve to be shared. This is less difficult when grandparents are able to spend a generous amount of time with their grandchil-dren. Today the incidence of family mobility and divorce combine with conflicting child-and-grandparent schedules to minimize the time available for being together. The grandparents' sharing of actual experiences becomes even more valuable in building family roots and relationships.

It is commonly assumed that grandparents will take the lead in orienting their grandchildren to family history. We further suppose the young are naturally interested in learning about their origins. One caution should be noted, however. Until children reach a particular level of reasoning ability, usually at about age twelve or thirteen, they cannot understand distant time. For this reason, most of the family stories directed to preteenagers should center on the childhood experiences of their own parents. Arizona State University's program for grandparents provides lists of recommended story topics and ways to introduce them. The plan notes that youngsters can get to know their parents better by finding out what they were like as children. Grandparents still remember those days, so they are probably the best source of information. Besides these details, there may be other questions a grandparent can answer:

- What kinds of things made you proud of Mom [or Dad]?
- What were some of the silly things Mom [or Dad] did with friends?
- What jobs did Mom [or Dad] say they would like as adults?
- What was the worst thing Mom [or Dad] ever did?

Developing Self-Concept through Shared Stories

The conditions for effective storytelling have changed, especially since, years ago, most children were expected to be seen and not heard. They were frequently reminded of their duty to respect older people, an obligation which included listening attentively (and silently) whenever grandparents told stories. More recently, society has decided that persons of every age group deserve respect. (In some circles this amounts to freedom without responsibility!) This conviction is reinforced in school, where teachers attempt to promote favorable self-concept—the view that everyone is unique and special.

Given this orientation, it is not surprising that young people consider events in their lives to be just as important as the events reported by grown-ups. The resulting behavior can easily be misunderstood—what may seem to be a lack of deference towards adults can also be interpreted as a demand for equality. Since the right to be heard is fundamental to equality, the experiences of grandparents deserve to be told—but, theoretically, so do the grandchildren's experiences. Mutual storytelling enables both generations to understand and respect each other. In all of this, we must emphasize that parents and grandparents would do well to motivate greater respect and attention and to lovingly, tactfully, and firmly insist upon them.

There are themes known to interest children at specified age levels. Topics such as dating, school, sports, money, religion, and vocational aspiration provide excellent opportunities for storytelling. The following questions for grandparents, to be slightly reworded as necessary when directed to grandchildren, illustrate the content of shared stories about experiences at school.

- How were kids punished when you went to school?
- What do you remember about life in the classroom?
- What was your greatest fear while at school?
- How did you feel about homework and report cards?
- What was your favorite activity in school?
- How did you feel about your teachers?

Volunteer Grandparents

Successful home-school parents often adopt grandparents when their own are not around or when they lack sound values or teaching aptitude. This can greatly enrich young lives—primarily when the grandparents are retired but want to continue their responsibility and usefulness to society.

The need to enrich life while we try to prolong it is the goal of various groups which place older volunteers in the community. Perhaps the best known organization is RSVP, an acronym for the Retired Senior Volunteers Program. The men and women who take part in this nationwide program want to learn how to make the best use of an overabundance of leisure time, how to retain a sense of pride in themselves and how to enjoy rather than resent the years which remain. RSVP places individuals in nonprofit settings such as hospitals, libraries and schools. The grandparents in this program are especially urged to volunteer their time for families and schools.

With RSVP in the classroom, elderly volunteers perform such tasks as checking homework, listening to students read, shelving books in the library, and facilitating discussions in social studies. In return for these efforts, the volunteers have much to gain, since the stimulation of interaction with children helps prevent loneliness and depression. They can also do the same in the home school, especially when parents are forced to work. By directly helping youngsters, seniors can favorably revise the common idea that older people are a selfish group who want respect without responsibility. For the 80 percent of elderly persons who are grandparents, volunteering at school or home presents an opportunity to learn more about the age group of their own grandchildren.

Wherever possible, grandparents should have a well-defined constructive role in society and the family, particularly among those who are able to school at home. Before this transition can take place, however, many grandparents may need access to creative educational programs that can make them and their children comfortable in a larger family relationship. Some customary grandparental practices may have to be revised, yet all concerned may expect significant positive changes when they develop mutual respect. Children, while learning this respect, must be taught to honor both parents and grandparents—if we who are grandparents are to be taken seriously as models. In turn, we will try to deserve to be honored and will recognize the need to understand our children's views—and how they develop—as a precondition for expressing our own. For grandparents, this may be more difficult these days, but the personal growth it requires can also mean that the grandparent experience may be richer, happier, and more worthwhile than ever before.

V. Professional Relationships

20.   Satellites: Home and School Working Together

A YEAR OR SO ago one of America's leading Christian school officials expressed chagrin to me that we would endorse home schooling. His schools were losing students. I asked him if he had considered cooperating with home schools. He demurred. But the other day, a year or two later, we learned that he has become a home school enthusiast. He had decided to place children's needs ahead of enrollments, and he had learned more about satellites.

One of the simplest legal alternatives to public or private school is the satellite, or "adjunct home school," as it might be called, where the established traditional school (public, private, or parochial) and the home school work together. Such a plan may be particularly helpful or necessary if your state law is stringent. When the possibility of adjunct home schools in association with a private school was suggested recently by a home-schooling attorney to one commissioner of education and his legal counsel, they recognized the potential validity of such schools under their state law.

Institutional teachers often make good coaches for home-schoolers. Educators most likely to cooperate are those who understand the superiority of a caring home over the best of institutions. The fact that many professionals—including public school administrators—conduct home schools for their own children is evidence that the idea is not altogether rejected by highly educated people. Relatively few school officials will harass family schools, since research has clearly shown the value of the home as the best nest during the children's early years. Educators who know the United States Constitution generally also believe in the parents' prior right to choose the education of their own children—under the First Amendment, as determined by a series of United States Supreme Court decisions dating back to 1925.[1] Still other educators take note of determined parents and their beautifully home-schooled children and reason, "If you can't beat them, join them."

Home Schools Take Many Forms

1. The parents determine instructional methods and curriculum without outside formal or institutional help, purchasing instructional materials from various sources.

2. The children are enrolled in a specific curriculum or customized system of instruction from an organization or school, which may be at the other end of the continent. This institution may have many such satellite home schools—hundreds or even thousands scattered over the globe. In some cases, this arrangement provides a legal umbrella for the home school, but in others such affiliation is ignored by officials. An example of this plan is the Hewitt-Moore Child Development Center in Washougal, Washington. Whatever program you choose for this purpose, we urge you to keep in mind the principles set forth in this book, as well as in our *Home-Grown Kids* and *Home-Spun Schools.* The best home-school curricula provide work-study balance, minimize workbooks and daily formal teaching, customize curricula for each child, help parents in dealing with the state, give formal studies only to children ages eight to ten or older, and concentrate on stories that are true for reading material.

3. The home school is attached to a local private, public, or church school—which provides supervision and legal coverage for a small fee. It may or may not supply materials.

4. Some public school districts actually enroll home-schoolers as regular students and claim state aid for them, offering whatever

help the parents want, but affirming parental rights to teach in their own way.

The children may be officially enrolled at the school they might eventually attend. The parent acts as instructional aide and carries out a program appropriate to the age level of the child. In one large city system of Christian schools a knowledgeable leader conducts group meetings for home-schooling parents on a regular basis to help and encourage them in their program. Such a support group provides mutual sharing of ideas and the opportunity for fellowship with like-minded people whether the child is too young for academic work or is eight or older and ready for formal at-home schooling.

Many public schools provide teacher-coaches for home-schooling parents. These professionals generally find that there is little for them to do—because of the aptness of the parents and the naturalism of the home education situation. One large church not only provides a Christian school for its members but also employs a consultant to work with twenty-five home schools within the congregation. In this case, most of the children are in an informal kindergarten-type program. A number of other Christian schools are also considering such a plan.

The degree to which parents—and their adjunct schools—depend upon these "mother" institutions varies. Some centers provide all materials and weekly supervision. Others simply make available their advice and resources—libraries, enrichment classes, and so on—as parents ask for them. Some public schools include such "enrollments" in reports to their counties or states, receiving the same level of state subsidy as for regular public school students. Some schools have traveling teachers who, in fact, become educators as they provide counsel to home-schooling parents.

Guidelines for Satellite Arrangements

Interestingly enough, there is yet no research evidence which distinguishes the "supervised" parents from those who are more independent. Nor is there any suggestion that parents who are trained teachers do better than those who are not. While some of the greatest home teaching is done by highly trained parents, we find that professional teachers are among the most doubtful of their ability to educate their own children. Their attitude is much like that of a surgeon who seldom wants to operate on his or her own family. The keys to good home teaching, we repeat, are warm responsiveness, and consistency of adult example—not heavy exposure to books, helpful as they may be.

• Both satellite and supervising schools must understand and protect the prior rights of the parents to determine the education of their children as guaranteed by the First Amendment to the Constitution and interpreted by the U.S. Supreme Court in a series of decisions over the past 60 or 70 years. They also need to recognize the state's obligation to see that the child's health, safety and basic educational requirements are met, including preparation for good citizenship.

• Both parties should understand the philosophy, purpose, nature and outcomes of an optimum satellite. For instance:

1. The best teaching is by example, and parents are therefore teaching literally all day, all year.

2. There should be no formal classes until eight to ten years of age.[2] Until then, using the ideas given in the books, *Home-Grown Kids* and *Home-Spun Schools,* plus some imagination, will build the kind of foundation on which book learning can succeed best.

3. Warm, consistent, positive responses are by far the most effective teaching device. On a one-to-one basis, the parent has a wide advantage over even the best-prepared teacher, even though the parent may not be college-educated. Furthermore, parents do not have to cope with a wide variety of childhood backgrounds and behavior as do regular teachers. Handicapped children may sometimes be exceptions, yet they perhaps need consistent parental responses most of all.

4. In a one-to-one arrangement, the parents can easily teach as much or more in a total of sixty to ninety minutes of instruction, with a like amount of supervised study, as the school would normally provide in a full school day in more than twice that time.

5. The child should spend the remainder of his "school day"—about the same time period as for study—helping his parent(s) in productive manual work, possibly in a cottage industry (now becoming so popular), and in service to his neighbors, the ill, aged, and others who might need help. This does not bar play, but gives greater emphasis to productive work and the building of skills as the child develops. If a child starts to work when he starts to walk and learns to put away his toys before he is taken for a stroll, by the time he is eight or ten he should be able to do almost anything around the home.

6. Normally, the satellite child will be receiving a balanced education and learning to be a producer, and his parents will focus on giving him more tools than toys and encouraging work and service rather than amusements and sports.

• The satellite and the school should agree on:

1. Broad goals for the child—reading, writing, arithmetic, citizenship, and so on.
2. The means for annual evaluation.
3. The time(s) and method of periodic checks.
4. The charges, if any, for this limited service.
5. The bases upon which the child will be received into regular school, if and when he enrolls.
6. Minimal controls and supervision, within the Constitution's constraints.

• The satellite should choose its own curriculum, without compulsion or undue direction from the school, as long as the satellite's overall ideals are sound and comparable with normal school goals. This should be determined before the agreement is concluded, but the parents should have a sense of being in charge.

• When and if the satellite child does enroll full-time in an institutional school, he should normally be placed with his agemates, and not measured by the number of years in school or workbooks or courses of study completed. Generally, he will have competencies, skills, and understandings which schools usually do not supply. These should be balanced against academic skills, which—in the unlikely event that a child is short in any subject—will usually come quickly and easily to him.

21. Making the Transition from Home School to Regular School or Formal Study

PAT GRAYBILL of Loveland, Colorado, called us in alarm shortly after she decided to transfer her home-schooled son to regular school. The church-school teacher was insisting that Bucky go through all the early grades before he could be placed in the grade for those of his age. Pat soon found that the teacher knew little about child development and had the popular idea that if a child missed a formal grade, his life would not be complete. We advised that the teacher be given some basic materials on children, and be asked to evaluate the boy objectively. When this teacher finally discovered that Bucky Graybill was actually achieving above others of his age, and she had read a book on child development, she acted like a new woman, and began "educating" other teachers.

There are enough tradition-bound teachers that some parents have reason to worry. Parents are often puzzled about how to help their child make the transition from informal learning, acquired before ages eight to ten, to formal studies thereafter. Although we strongly urge that your child be entered eventually with his age-mates, don't be in a hurry to institutionalize him. The more we see of the excellence of home-schooling, the more we encourage parents to keep it up as long as they can handle it. Just decide one year at a time.

It does not matter how extensive your own education has been.

We know good parent-teachers who do not have high school diplomas. The keys are (a) keeping ahead of your child in the basic skills; (b) using your imagination to make the best of every learning opportunity; (c) obtaining sound curriculum materials; (d) using your local library; (e) being warm, responsive parents, and as consistent as possible. This last item, as a one-to-one experience with your child, is teaching that no regular school can match.

If you must send your child to school, try to find an ungraded primary classroom or a teacher who understands individualized methods. (Or educate the teachers as Pat Graybill did. She used our book *Better Late Than Early;* others use *School Can Wait.*)

Your eight-year-old should be placed with his age-mates— probably in the second or third grade (a twelve-year-old belongs between the sixth and eighth)—depending on his birthdate, size, and overall maturity. For example, a twelve-year-old may be closer to eleven than thirteen. He should never be *labeled* a first-grader, whatever his actual age. If he has not had any formal training, he may have to be started with first-grade materials in the 3 *R*'s. Remedial teachers often find that children, usually boys, have been started to school too early and even after two or three years are still not ready for anything more difficult than first-grade material for the basics of reading, writing, and arithmetic. When they are mature enough, they will move rapidly through the books, usually requiring little of the repetition needed by younger children. Subject matter such as social studies, science, and religion can be learned right along with the class.

Truly professional teachers not only readily accept such children without protest, but also welcome the opportunity to work with the typically mature child who comes from a responsive home situation. It is a sad fact that some teachers are frustrated because they understand neither how children develop nor the basic principles of teaching—how to start where the child is and proceed at his rate of maturity. They teach subjects or classes, not *children.* Others are prejudiced because you have not trusted your little ones earlier to the "professionals." They consider parents incompetent to do anything with their own children besides care for them physically. We often intercede for parents when schools insist on starting older children in the first grade. Rapid book learning is not at all phenomenal for late starters who were free to explore during their early years without the oppressive rigidity of the classroom.

Suppose your daughter is eight in January or February. Up to this point she has had no book learning as such. You have read to her consistently from her very early months. You have followed a program similar to that suggested in *Home-Grown Kids* and have learned to enjoy her as she matures. She has been saturated with practical knowledge gained from working with you and from opportunities to explore nature. She knows her alphabet and her numbers. She can count to 100 by 1's, 2's, 5's and 10's (she likely progressed in that order). You have played sound and rhyming games with her and have sung to her and with her. She has memorized poems, verses, and finger plays. In a sense, she has been "reading" since birth—reading your face, your smile, and later, pictures, letters, and words. Now she really wants to (and can) learn to read formally and thoughtfully. So why not teach her?

Get a set of materials from a publisher or curriculum center that provides sound instructional programs.[1] Start out with perhaps twenty or thirty minutes at first, gradually working up to an hour or two a day, depending on her interest. She won't need as much repetition as a six-year-old and should not be bogged down with "busy work" of the sort often given to first-graders in school. Your daughter will probably progress so fast it will astound you. *This is the miracle of readiness.* She has learned to reason consistently and is capable of thinking things through for herself. In other words, she is "cognitively" ready. She will probably be more than ready for third grade in the fall (at age eight, if you really want to let her go). On the other hand, if she shows no interest in sounds, words, reading, and writing (or if your child is a boy), you would probably be wise to delay school entry. Many parents today are teaching at home throughout the elementary grades and, increasingly, even through high school.

Be especially careful if you have a boy, unless he shows definite maturity for school-type learning. Boys are more likely to be in the nine-to-ten-year range before they are ready for formal study. But they thrive on practical ventures, on making and selling things *with you,* or visiting and helping those in need! (We make suggestions for such projects in *Home-Grown Kids.*) Consider forming a family industry, such as Smith & Son, and make him an officer. This is great for arithmetic and the development of both character and personality.

As you prepare the transition to regular school, don't fail to have a regular weekly time to help those who are less fortunate! Work and service make great kids! When they do go to school, they will be leaders socially and behaviorally as well as academically. They will not be bound by their peers, but will get along with and respect adults. Such children become self-directed, productive, patriotic citizens. They are much more likely to have a sense of self-worth and will do things simply because they are intrinsically good. Schooled at home wisely, they reason maturely, unburned by the social contagion of the peer-dependent culture which is found in most institutional schools.

22. How Far Shall We Submit to State Control?

IN THE EARLY 1950s, shortly after World War II, we went to Japan to reorganize an American-Japanese College. We had determined in advance that the school would hold to certain principles which were not consistent with the Japanese-Shinto education ethic. Besides, we were setting up a work-study program in a culture that had little use for manual training for college students, yet our program would take several hours from daily study time. Few of our teachers were certified by the government, and the regulations required that we be accredited if we were going to educate teachers. The Japan Ministry of Education would not accredit us directly because of our philosophy.

We went to one university after another, seeking accreditation by affiliation. Some officials smiled sympathetically; others expressed pity. But none would help us until we finally went to Tamagawa University, Tokyo's leading teacher-education institution. Many years earlier, when he was a student at the University of Illinois, Tamagawa's Dean Tsunekichi Mizuno had read of the balanced education we proposed and apparently liked our inclination to experiment. So he agreed to have Tamagawa affiliate with us.

Dr. Mizuno had high standing in Japan as the former head of all religious and social education at Japan's Ministry of Education. Yet his professors opposed him, and when all twelve of

176

our pilot group failed the Tamagawa entrance examinations, they ridiculed him. But he stood his ground.

Our early failure later proved to be a great advantage, for it proved that we had not selected only our top students to demonstrate our theory of balance between work and study. To further test us, the Tamagawa classes were taught by our teachers to the twelve students, who worked physically an average of more than twenty hours weekly. Although papers were graded by the hostile Tamagawa professors, when the first semester grades came out, our students had earned 106 *A*'s, 57 *B*'s and 6 *C*'s. At the end of their fourth year, all twelve passed, *ten of them with A-plus averages.* All, of course, were granted teaching certificates. This taught us something about the wisdom, character, and courage of educators like Dr. Mizuno.

Is Credentialing Necessary?

Even literature from the liberal Brookings Institution, one of the world's eminent think tanks, sheds doubt on the cost-effectiveness of those popular accreditation exercises which have come to be regarded as sacred in Western education. Such credentialing and policing may be necessary for professional schools—law, medicine, nursing, where lives may be at stake—but no objective educator will insist on their necessity for general education. Remember, as you read this chapter, that *all* research studies on home schools have shown them to be superior to institutional schools. We have seen that parents' success as teachers depends not on their amount of parental education but on their warmth and responsiveness, salted with common sense.

Whether or not the fault can be laid at the institutional door, two things are true about certification standards: the longer they have been applied to general education, the more it has declined; and the more controls we have, the less freedom American education has had for exploring freely. The result has been a steady decline in literacy for over a century. If this is true, why do we worship these requirements and encourage the state controls which largely feed on them?

There is also a possible lapse of integrity here, as well as a great deal of conflict of interest and many remarkable inconsistencies. The National Education Association (NEA), which is so protective of some rigid controls, is actually afraid of merit pay—which would require its teachers to be measured. And if this happened, where would its seniority system be? Executives of NEA and the American Federation of Teachers (AFT) gesture for excellence, yet try to destroy home schools—the only classrooms which consistently surpass their own institutions. The NEA has not yet accepted our challenge to conduct studies which compare home schools with other schools. Yet what alternatives does it offer? If it would only cooperate with home education, it would be taking a long leap toward excellence in education.

Consider the recent statement of the eminent professor Jacques Barzun in the *New York Review of Books:* "The once proud and efficient public school system of the United States has turned into a wasteland where violence and vice share the time with ignorance and idleness." [1] This is a far cry from the original intentions of accreditation and certification in the United States—which were directed primarily toward insuring the ascendancy of the church. Now the state has turned the tables and in many cases has all but taken over parental rights. If you doubt that this is true, look—from Hawaii and California to North Dakota and Nebraska, and from New York and Florida to New Mexico and Nevada—at those who at this writing are trying to seize control of the children in the name of sound education. If public education were sound and the home schools were doing an inferior job, there might be some basis for such thinking. But for inferior state schools to try to pull down the productive home school is an astonishing exercise in deception.

This reminds us of Aleksandr Solzhenitsyn, Russian Nobel Laureate, who observed that Russians were "being arrested and tried, not for their actual faith, but for openly declaring their convictions and for bringing up their children in the same spirit." [2] The same actions that were specified as political crimes under Russia's Article 58–10 of the Marxist Code are precisely the same as we now see operating in many of the fifty states. The

U.S.S.R.-oriented Tolstoy Foundation in New York suggests also that all Soviet Christians want to leave Russia for the same reasons, the principal one being their desire to teach their children without breaking the law.[3] Noted Finnish home economist Annikki Suviranta declares that we are already well on the way to totalitarianism.

Even some of our most notorious agnostics of the past would turn over in their graves if they witnessed the prosecution and persecution of many parents today by state agencies and their public school personnel and social workers. Listen to the measure of state control laid down by John Stuart Mill: "An education established and controlled by the state should only exist, if it exists at all, as one among many competing experiments, carried on for the purpose of example and stimulus, to keep the others up to a certain standard of excellence." [4]

Educating the Legislators

The schools of any nation are not going to improve by trying to destroy those who exceed their performance—as teacher unions and their compatriots have been trying to do. Commenting upon New Mexico's discrediting of home instruction as "a private school," Assistant Attorney General Scott D. Spencer of New Mexico's State Department of Education observed that home instruction "violates the New Mexico compulsory school attendance law, and will subject parents to criminal prosecution." [5] In answer to an inquiry we made on behalf of a number of New Mexico constituents, he retorted: "Recently, the New Mexico Court of Appeals upheld the constitutionality of that law and the convictions of two parents who were teaching children at home. While we respect your right to your opinion, the people of the state of New Mexico, who elect the legislators who make our laws, disagree with you." [6]

In every state where parents and legislators are fully informed, the home has enjoyed substantial freedom. Mr. Spencer and those who believe as he does must be helped to understand the true needs of children and the rights of parents and the excellence of their combination in the home school. Such doubters should be taught the folly of present certification trends. As has been shown in a number of states in the last few years, this can be best done by educating those who elect the legislators. If you prize your freedoms, those of you who are reading this book must pass on your information and convictions to those who make your laws so that they will legislate in harmony with your children's verified needs and your historical rights as guaranteed by the United States Constitution.

Unfortunately, not only public school officials and social workers disagree with us. Many pastors and church school leaders are among the fiercest opponents of family schools—either because of tradition or fear of student loss. This onslaught of attacks by institutions against the home is not a case of the "pot calling the kettle black," for the record of the home school is too clean. It is, rather, the "lion labeling the lamb dangerous." Your response to this charade will determine the cultural and moral level of this land.

Fortunately, the attitudes of many church and public educators are changing. But there is still a long way to go. We need some reminders about what good education really is and the necessary limitations of schools, for few really have a deep and broad understanding of the educational process. Many programs and institutions are appropriate as our servants, but far from desirable as our masters. We must retrace our steps, reflect on what has happened, and allocate teaching to its most productive niche. It is time to decide, on the basis of fact rather than tradition, who does the best, and to discover why and how and when and where we determine quality.

What Makes a "Quality" Teacher?

There are many great teachers, but most of the best do not know they are. They are so in awe of their educational responsibility that they often doubt their own excellence. As we noted earlier, professional teachers who are trained to handle *groups* of children, but who decide to school their own children at home, tend to be more fearful than lay persons without professional training. Good teachers are so busy responding to the questions and needs of others that they have not had time to measure themselves carefully. The possibility of their greatness does not occur to them. In the ranks of quality teachers are mothers, fathers, ministers, schoolteachers, employers, supervisors and—children. In fact, children are often the greatest teachers of all, both by precept and by example.

To talk responsibly about teaching forces us, first, to quash some widely cherished myths and, second, to offer some truths that some will not like and which certification standards find hard to measure. The highest level of teaching, for instance, whether at home or school, reflects general factors seldom considered by the state. Yet, as we shall explain later, this is not necessarily the teacher's fault.

The top teacher is not a didactic, pedantic pedagogue, sheltered from the students by a big desk which often is no-man's-land. The best teacher, regardless of certification, is the one who is aware of the crucial interaction of adult and child feelings, and who provides a responsive, understanding, inspiring, emotional sanctuary for the students. Thus, most of the spectacular teaching results we have seen in nearly fifty professional years have involved both rural and urban parents, mainly without college degrees and usually without much confidence—but with a lot of love. Scattered in all states of the Union, most of them hold certain qualities in common: warm hearts and responsive lips, the courage of their moral convictions, and love for their country and their God—in whom they trust.

In 1977, Vicki Rice, without a college education, brought her failing daughter, Leslie Sue, up nearly three grades in about nine months, teaching her about one and one-half hours a day. (This story and others are more fully told in *Home-Spun Schools.*) In western New York, after the Douglas Orts and four other families taught their seven children in their homes a few hours daily, the seven averaged in the top 10 percent of the Stanford Achievement Tests, and three of them in the top 1 percent. In Forest Falls, California, Marge Schafer had little confidence in her ability to teach her children, yet felt forced to do so because of failure and other psychosocial symptoms related to their schooling. So she and her husband, Dick, took their two failing boys out of school—one acutely hyperactive, the other with dangerous withdrawal tendencies—and turned them into excellent scholars and outgoing social leaders in their community and church.

The Roland E. Morrows were taken to court in Grand Island, Nebraska, on charges of criminal child neglect. One child was retarded since birth but was distinctly improving in the Morrow home school. But the *certified* teacher of the retarded child protested that he was not getting enough television and therefore was suffering "neglect." She did not mention—and perhaps did not know—that a child of this sort profits little from such contrived adult fantasies. The teacher was actually recommending an educational prescription which was precisely what the youngster did not need. The other Morrow child, a daughter, was in the top 13 percent nationally in her schoolwork. As is usually the case, Dorothy Morrow's teaching remarkably surpassed the work of the local professionals.

The happiest note is that these are not exceptions. They are typical of families who realize that all schools should strive for excellence, that the home is *the basic school* and crucial to all others, and that institutions cannot be truly excellent without sound homes.

Most of these families watched little or no television, and all the children had to work a good deal. But most of all they had parents who cared and who provided a clear set of family values. These are the key factors in both city and country. If parents do not have these qualities and concerns, and are unwilling or unable to develop them, they should not school their own.

What we have said in this book certainly does not depreciate all school teachers nor does it put down our schools. It does face the fact that classroom teachers have handicaps which parents do not usually have to face. Accordingly, it suggests that great teaching must not be fenced in by certificates, degrees, or the National Education Association—whose preoccupation with teacher certification seems far more an exercise in union job control than a gesture toward fine teaching or a concern for children. Teaching credentials not only provide little assurance of skill, but often protect the worst kind of educators. For example, they give no guarantee of fine character and personality, even though adult example is one of teaching's most productive tools.

Good teaching is the inevitable harvest of love, as exemplified by Marge Schafer's retrieval of her children. Most of the families mentioned lived away from big cities. City schools have it harder, as do city families, too. City schools carry the same burdens and handicaps as city homes.

Educators and classroom specialists sometimes grasp the importance of their calling. When they do not, they teach "by the seat of their pants," as they were taught—with little attention to pertinent research and a pitiful lack of original thought. They are less thinkers than reflectors of others' ideas, although they worry little about how others thought in the first place. They may be licensed, certified, credentialed and have a string of degrees after their names, yet totally miss the point of their profession—to enrich the lives of their students to the highest possible level. Parents and teachers who doubt their own abilities—but who love children—should take courage.

Those who demand certification for home schools fail to realize not only the advantages of the one-to-one tutorial system, but also the difficulty the parent-teacher does not have to face: the classroom teacher must usually account for the variables of twenty or thirty or more children—their diverse backgrounds and home situations, their wide range of abilities and values. It is the necessity for handling these variables that is primarily used to justify teacher-education programs and certification. The tutorial program does not need such special training. In the face of the record, if anyone can provide you with a series of sound, sensible, or research-based reasons for certification which offset the fine records of the home schools, please seize him and get us the evidence. We will pay you well!

23. Home Schools and the Law

WE RECEIVE calls daily from home-schooling parents who are involved in court cases or have unfounded fears of impending problems. Many feel threatened by inquiries from school districts, family "protective" services, police departments, district attorneys, and sometimes by neighbors or even close relatives who report them. For this reason, we have been careful to take counsel from lawyers, prosecutors, judges, and legislators in order to simplify the many complex factors that often surround such cases. In turn, we help to orient and educate lawyers and judges—individually and in groups. However, we have found that only about one out of ten of these troubled parents is actually the target of civil or criminal action. And less than one out of ten of these goes to court. Of those cases that do go to court, we are thus far winning about 90 percent. (For more detailed discussion on the law and actual court summations, see *Home-Spun Schools.*)

The Constitution, as interpreted in a sequence of decisions by the United States Supreme Court over more than sixty years, guarantees parents the prior right to determine the education of their children. Any state policies or laws in conflict with this principle are unconstitutional and therefore un-American. Some authorities describe them as "totalitarian," which in fact they are when control of children is superimposed by the state instead of coming from those who are their parents.

The compelling rights of the state include the power to require that children have at least the literacy we would require of an immigrant before he is granted citizenship. The state may expect minimum literacy skills—reading, writing, arithmetic—and a knowledge of our government for good citizenship. It may also require reasonable standards of health and safety. Fortunately, the home school is usually best at providing all of these. (By a home school, we mean *concerned parents, teaching their children systematically at home.*)

Basic Principles: Preparing Your Case

1. It is important that you have clear, informed convictions right from the start and that you be strong in those convictions. Otherwise, there is no opportunity for even a test. A preference is one thing; a conviction is entirely another. When Jon Bailey was legal counsel for the Indiana State Board of Education, he told district superintendents who were dealing with home-schooling parents, "Test them if you want to, but if they are firm in their convictions, leave them alone if you don't want trouble and potential embarrassment."

2. It is crucial to know your rights as citizens, and your privileges and responsibilities under the United States Constitution. This was spelled out clearly in *Home-Spun Schools,* and we have included the same information here as Appendix B.

3. Decide which is more important to you: integrity and principle, or conventional wisdom and practice. Stated another way, you must first decide whether you are really more concerned about the needs of your children than the pressures of your neighbors and others in society or sometimes even in your job. This is a real test of your values and even your character.

4. At the earliest possible point in your home-schooling experience, you should seek counsel from the best informed people you can find. When we at the Hewitt Research Foundation are informed *early enough* to handle the matter tactfully and professionally with school superintendents, we usually are able to persuade them that court action is not in the best interests of children

and is therefore not professional. (The Hewitt staff is, of course, committed first to those who are Associates of the Foundation. But we are working to prepare personnel to help all who are in need.) Also, because of legal precedents and their poor chance of winning, we suggest to officials that it would not be profitable to pursue action against home-schooling parents. However, once agencies, particularly the so-called family "protective" services, commit themselves to action, it is much more difficult to dissuade them from it.

5. It is important to find the best possible legal assistance if you are actually faced with an arraignment, court hearing, or trial—procedures usually pursued by the state in that order. We have made a start on a roster of skilled, successful, sympathetic, and knowledgeable lawyers. Eventually we expect to cover every state. Some are truly expert, proven attorneys who are willing and able to counsel nationally. If such top experts are not in your state, you can work through lawyers who are so licensed. A few top lawyers have handled home-school cases outside their own states by working through local attorneys. Many have also made themselves available for counsel to other attorneys and/ or clients from another state, often without cost. We must be careful not to overload these generous people.

6. Be cautious in your actual selection of an attorney. A number of parents have made the mistake of choosing an attorney at random instead of determining whether or not the lawyer is sympathetic to home schools or if he is well-acquainted with constitutional law as it pertains to education. We cannot overemphasize this point! Again and again, parents have retained lawyers or have been assigned public defenders who had little sympathy for their clients, lacked interest in obtaining knowledge on home schools, or were more concerned about money than truth. Some attorneys fear loss of business if they appear to be going against the public school, and may actually seem to work against the parents. Because of this possibility, Roland Morrow handled his own case in Central City, Nebraska. Yet, it is preferable that you have a lawyer, if possible.

We urge that, whenever possible, you see that your lawyer,

who may be making a real sacrifice to help home-school parents, receives his or her full pay. It is always a good idea to shop carefully for your lawyer, in terms of fees as well as skill. Some lawyers have charged heavily for "studying up" on home schools, or have stretched cases out unconscionably. Unnecessary delays result when a lawyer gives higher priority to other business or does not make the urgency of the case clear to the court. (We do not refer here to judicial delays beyond the control of the attorney.) Remember, though, that the cheapest lawyer may not be the best, and the best may be the cheapest in the long run. Some sympathetic attorneys often make special allowance for home-schoolers.

For some of the reasons above, we at Hewitt often find it necessary to educate lawyers about home schools, including the professional and constitutional aspects, as well as research bases and legal briefs. This is the reason we have included a chapter on parents and the law in our book *Home-Spun Schools*. There we document an extensive series of legal briefs—cases which have been successful in court or in which we obtained dismissal before trial. Santa Monica Attorney Michael Smith recently observed that this book was all a lawyer needed to handle a home-school case. Even now, we are receiving home-school legal monographs from lawyers in a number of states, including Georgia, Nebraska, and Texas. Home-school cases are so diverse that attorneys may choose to take other routes than we suggest. But we must reemphasize the importance of carefully evaluating the ability, sympathy, and knowledgeability of your prospective lawyer with respect to home-schooling. Also compare their fees. The best attorneys tend to cost the least because they handle cases more efficiently. To this end, *ensure that your lawyer is aware of other more experienced attorneys to whom he might go for counsel.* Many have now become expert on family-school relationships.

Most home-school cases are treated as criminal-child-neglect matters, yet these generally are easier to defend because the state is put in the position of having to prove its case. More difficult is truancy, a civil case. Here again, a great deal depends upon the attitude, experience and skill of your lawyer, his careful scholarship in preparing your case, his willingness to counsel with others and the respect he has earned in court.

Types of Courts and Trials

It also makes considerable difference whether or not you are tried in a local court—one that is not a Court of Record. Such courts seem to be far more capricious than the higher courts. They are also to be less feared, because you can usually ask later for a trial in the Court of Record—just as the Rices did, as noted in *Home-Spun Schools.*

Once a person gets to the Court of Record, there is also the matter of whether the trial will be by judge only or by jury. In at least two of the twenty or more cases in which we have borne witness, the request for a jury trial was crucial. In both cases— Blankenship in Atlanta and Morrow in Central City, Nebraska— some thought before the trial that the judges and prosecutors were working too closely together to insure objectivity. The jury in each case reportedly sensed the efforts of the prosecutor to obstruct truth and quickly gave us favorable decisions.

One current option is the right of the parents to sue the state and/or its officials under the Civil Rights Act (CRA), Sections 1983, 1985, 1986, 1988, of 42 U.S. code, etc. (see Appendix G of *Home-Spun Schools*). In such a suit, if successful, the CRA provides for reimbursement of your lawyer. Don't overwork this approach, but take care also not to overlook it.

If you do have any premonition of trouble or think that you are going to be threatened in any way, it is highly advisable that you have with you throughout any pertinent conversations a witness other than someone from your own family. If such witnessed conversations or any correspondence sent to you by public officials contain any threat—fine, imprisonment, loss of children, or other well-defined harassment—we are advised that you may have a basis for suit. A few aggressive actions under the Civil Rights statutes have already become strong deterrents to public officials bent on harassing parents.

A leading Minneapolis lawyer recently wrote us of a Federal

District Court case in Minnesota that involved a verdict in excess of one million dollars for a county's actions in deprivation of civil rights under Section 1983. In this case the parents were reportedly accused by a county welfare agency. The judgment was later reduced to $260,000, but has served its purpose of keeping public officials more cautious about random prosecution of citizens.

Be Prepared

You must be thoroughly informed! Some attorneys tell us that our books will be of great help if carefully read. You will also be stronger after having supported others in their legal problems. If you have weak convictions or are merely expedient, you have less likelihood of winning. This is no time to run away and hide, but a time to be firm, kind, tactful—and very strong and well-informed. Paranoia wins few battles. One dear mother, deeply convicted but misguided, got herself ordained into a "Mother Earth Church" for $10.00. We could not defend her under these circumstances, for her action smacked of the diploma-mill game. Principle and truth are more effective in court than such good-intentioned ploys. Other parents have been inconsistent, stubborn, or even downright rude. We do not need battle axes in this war. Firmness in the right, as God leads us to see the right, is much more likely to succeed.

We also find it hard to defend parents who are sloppy, disorganized, unclean in their persons and around their homes, or discourteous and unrefined in manner or language. Disorderliness does not win cases. We come across very few such home-schooling parents, but when we do, our work is made almost impossible.

Knowing and Showing Your Legislators

Also important to mention, although it does not relate specifically to court, is the matter of knowing and helping your legislators. Most citizens seem to have little use for these officials or even knowledge of who they are and what they do. Some do not even know their representatives' names, and have not taken the trouble to vote one way or the other. In one sense, such citizens do not really deserve the rights that are guaranteed to them by the Constitution. We advise you not to be guilty of such indifference. It is important that you get acquainted with these men and women who represent you in the legislatures and keep in touch with the policies they pursue. (We will soon have a monograph on how to deal with legislatures.)

You must make your position very clear to them with respect to the family, your children, and the schools. It is important to do this in a careful, tactful, logical way, backing up your conclusions not only with a sound understanding of your constitutional privileges, but also with data from reliable professional sources. This is one reason that we have done a great deal of research and have laid down many facts in our books *Better Late Than Early, School Can Wait* (designed for professionals), *Home-Grown Kids,* and *Home-Spun Schools.* If you prefer an even more current scholarly source, we suggest that you obtain a copy of the Winter 1983 *Teachers College Record* in which we have tried to lay out the issues respecting families and schools.*

We suggest that you also involve your neighbors and friends in your contacts with the legislators, so that your representatives at the state capital will realize that you are not alone in your convictions. We recently had a number of excellent examples of this kind of witness when laws or policies were changed or bad laws were defeated in such states as Arizona, Georgia, Montana, and Louisiana—by the efforts of a relatively few constituents.

---

* You may obtain the complete journal from Columbia University, Teachers College Record, Box 103, West 120th Street, New York, NY 10027, for about $6.00. Or if you want only our comprehensive monograph reprint, send a self-addressed, 37-cent stamped envelope and $2.00 to Hewitt, marked "T.C.R."

A Final Word

NO COMPLETE BOOK on principles and methods of teaching has ever appeared, so it has been with some concern that we have written *Home-Style Teaching*. We firmly believe, however, that if you reasonably follow the suggestions laid down in its pages, *you will be a better than average teacher*.

We remind you now of a few key points which depart from most modern teaching, yet are absolutes for great education. Ignoring them has cost our schools dearly and has exacted a high price from our homes.

Readiness. If children are formally educated before they are ready mentally, physically, and emotionally, they will be damaged.

Development. Few teachers understand how children develop, yet great teaching is impossible without this understanding.

Thinking. Learning to think is far more precious than getting an "A" on workbook facts.

Testing. Be respectful, even reverent, here. No child should be tested on achievement before he is ready.

Resources. In the classroom or at home, other children can be your best teachers.

Balance. The child is cheated of self-worth if he is not taught at least as much to work as to study and play.

Competition. The ideal of the Golden Rule applies here—working together—in contrast to the spirit prevalent in most team sports today: *I* win at *your* expense.

Certification. In *basic education,* this requirement was meant to ensure that teachers learn how to teach institutionally—with many children in the classroom—yet remains unproven even there. For home teaching it is sometimes a handicap.

Finally, the first education should be the harmonious development of the child's physical, mental, and spiritual powers. Providing warm and understanding responses to your children's "hearts" accomplishes far more than pressuring book knowledge into their minds. When you practice the first method, other learning follows naturally, and you will know great teaching.

NOTES

Introduction

1. P. D. Forgione and R. S. Moore, "The Rationales for Early Childhood Education Policy Making," prepared for the U.S. Office of Economic Opportunity under Research Grant No. 500–79–G–73/01 to the Hewitt Research Foundation, Berrien Springs, Michigan, 1975, ED 114 208.

2. D. R. Metcalf, "An Investigation of Cerebral Lateral Functioning and the EEG," report of a study made for the U.S. Office of Economic Opportunity under Research Grant No. 50079–G–73–02–1 to Hewitt Research Foundation, Berrien Springs, Michigan, 1975, ERIC No. pending.

3. R. D. Moon and R. S. Moore, "The Effect of Early School Entrance on the School Achievement and Attitudes of Disadvantaged Children," report of a study made for the U.S. Office of Economic Opportunity under Research Grant No. 50079–G–73/02 to the Hewitt Research Foundation, Berrien Springs, Michigan, 1975, ED 146 198. R. S. Moore et al., "Influences on Learning in Early Childhood," report of a study made for the U.S. Office of Economic Opportunity under Research Grant No. 50079–G–73/01 to the Hewitt Research Foundation, Berrien Springs, Michigan, 1975, ED 144 711.

4. See Appendix A.

5. See Appendix A.

Chapter 1

1. For examples, see appendix, *Home-Grown Kids* (Waco, TX: Word Books, 1983), pp. 241–48.

2. "Homework," National Education Research Division bulletin (Washington, DC: NEA), January 1958. Includes many other sources.

3. Matt. 7:12; Rom. 12:10, KJV.

Chapter 2

1. John Goodlad, "A Study of Schooling: Some Findings and Hypotheses," *Phi Delta Kappan* 64:7 (March 1983).

2. Harold McCurdy, "The Childhood Pattern of Genius," *Horizon*, May 1960, p. 38.

3. Mortimer Adler, *The Paideia Proposal* (New York: Macmillan, 1982).

4. Marcelle Geber, "The Psycho-Motor Development of African Chil-

dren in the First Year, and the Influence of Maternal Behavior," *Journal of Social Psychology* 47 (1958): 185–95.

5. Harold Skeels et al., "A Study of Environmental Stimulation: An Orphanage Preschool Project," *University of Iowa Studies in Child Welfare*, vol. 15, no. 4 (Iowa City: University of Iowa Press, 1938).

6. Mary Budd Rowe, "Wait Time and Rewards," *Journal of Research in Science Teaching* 11:2 (1974), pp. 81–94.

7. Benjamin Bloom, *All Our Children Learning* (New York: McGraw-Hill, 1980).

8. Urie Bronfenbrenner, *The Two Worlds of Childhood* (New York: Simon & Schuster, 1970).

9. McCurdy, "The Childhood Pattern of Genius."

Chapter 3

1. Deut. 6:6–9; Ps. 111:10; Prov. 22:6.

Chapter 4

1. L. P. Ullensvang, "Thirty Percent of Food Intake Is by Snacking: Food Consumption Patterns in the Seventies," *Vital Speeches of the Day* 36:240 (1 February 1970).

2. A. C. Guyton, *Textbook of Medical Physiology* (Philadelphia: W. B. Saunders, 1971), pp. 90, 17, 755, 863.

3. M. G. Hardinge, "Rest, Rest, Rest," *Life and Health,* August 1974.

Chapter 5

1. The Hewitt-Moore broadcast quality tape series is considered by many broadcasters and parents to be the best available, and has been carefully developed over many years to help you build a complete child. See Appendix A for ordering information.

Chapter 7

1. Studies by Forgione and Moore, Metcalf and Moore, Moon and Moore, and Moore *et al.,* cited in notes to Introduction.

2. Joseph Wepman, in speech before International Reading Association, Seattle, WA, May 1967. Also "The Modality Concept," in *Perception and Reading,* ed. H. K. Smith (Newark: International Reading Association, 1968), pp. 1–6.

3. "Adult Performance Level Project," University of Texas (Austin, TX: 1983).

4. R. S. Moore and Dorothy N. Moore, *Better Late Than Early*

(New York: Reader's Digest Press, 1975; reprint, Waco, TX: Hewitt-Moore Publishing, 1983).

5. Anne O'Keefe, "What Head Start Means to Families," Department of Health, Education, and Welfare publication no. (OHDS) 79-31129 (Washington, DC: U.S. Government Printing Office, 1979).

6. See Appendix A for how to obtain this excellent resource.

Chapter 10

1. 2 Cor. 10:12, KJV.

Chapter 11

1. Gunther Hildebrandt of the University of Marburg, speaking before the International Conference on Non-Related Science, Herdecke, Germany, 1973.

Chapter 13

1. See note 2, chapter 1.

Chapter 14

1. Adler, *The Paideia Proposal.*

Chapter 15

1. Bronfenbrenner, *The Two Worlds of Childhood,* p. 109.

2. Albert Bandura and A. Huston, "Identification as a Process of Incidental Learning," *Journal of Abnormal and Social Psychology* 63:311-18 (1961). Albert Bandura, D. Ross, and S. A. Ross, "Transmission of Aggression through Imitation of Aggressive Models," *Journal of Abnormal and Social Psychology* 52:575-82 (1961). Albert Bandura and R. H. Walters, *Social Learning and Personality Development* (New York: Holt, Rinehart & Winston).

Chapter 17

1. Wilson Riles, *Time,* July 26, 1971, p. 38.

2. For a thoroughly scholarly treatment of readiness for learning, read *Better Late Than Early* or *School Can Wait* by Raymond and Dorothy Moore (Waco, TX: Hewitt-Moore Publishing).

3. Arnold Gesell, *The Normal Child and Primary Education* (New York: Ginn & Co., 1912), pp. 118-19.

Chapter 18

1. Dale Farran, "Now for the Bad News," *Parents* Magazine, September 1982.
2. J. D. Unwin, *Sex and Culture* (Oxford University Press, 1932).
3. C. Zimmerman and M. Frampton, *Family and Society* (New York: Van Nostrand, 1947).
4. Further information is available from Hewitt Research Foundation. See Appendix A.

Chapter 20

1. Raymond S. and Dorothy Moore, *Home-Spun Schools* (Waco, TX: Word Books, 1982), pp. 147–81.
2. See *Better Late Than Early* or *School Can Wait* for detailed treatment of entrance age and research sources.

Chapter 21

1. See *Home-Spun Schools* by Raymond and Dorothy Moore for a list of criteria for selecting such materials. Or, send a self-addressed, stamped envelope to Hewitt-Moore Child Development Center, Box 9, Washougal, WA 98671, specifying "Curriculum."

Chapter 22

1. Jacques Barzun, "The Wasteland of American Education," *New York Review of Books,* 5 November 1981, p. 34.
2. Aleksandr Solzhenitsyn, *The Gulag Archipelago 1918–1956* (New York: Harper & Row, 1973), pp. 37–38.
3. Kevin Lynch, "Moscow's Defiant Christians," *Conservative Digest,* October 1979, p. 21.
4. Robert L. Cunningham, *Education Free and Public* (Wichita, KS: Center for Independent Education of Wichita Collegiate School), p. 1.
5. Personal letter to Raymond S. Moore, dated August 24, 1983.
6. Ibid.

APPENDIX A

PRODUCT AND RESOURCE INFORMATION

For all books and other products prepared by Raymond and Dorothy Moore and associates, including *Better Late Than Early, School Can Wait, Home-Grown Kids, Home-Spun Schools,* the *Moore-McGuffey Reader Series,* the *Winston Grammar Program,* the *Math-It* curriculum, and the character-story cassette tapes, contact your local bookstore or write to Hewitt-Moore Publishing Co., Box 9, Washougal, WA 98671.

For information on home schooling, support groups, specific legal matters, and details on becoming a Hewitt Research associate, write to Hewitt Research Foundation, Box 9, Washougal, WA 98671. Please enclose a long, self-addressed, stamped envelope.

APPENDIX B

CIVIL RIGHTS

42 U.S. CODE

§ 1983. Civil action for deprivation of rights

Every person who, under color of any statute, ordinance, regulation, custom, or usage, of any State or Territory or the District of Columbia, subjects, or causes to be subjected, any citizen of the United States or other person within the jurisdiction thereof to the deprivation of any rights, privileges, or immunities secured by the Constitution and laws, shall be liable to the party injured in an action at law, suit in equity, or other proper proceeding for redress. For the purposes of this section, any Act of Congress applicable exclusively to the District of Columbia shall be considered to be a statute of the District of Columbia.

R.S. § 1979; Pub.L. 96–170, §1, Dec. 29, 1979, 93 Stat. 1284.

§ 1985. Conspiracy to interfere with civil rights

Preventing officer from performing duties

(1) If two or more persons in any State or Territory conspire to prevent, by force, intimidation, or threat, any person from accepting or holding any office, trust, or place of confidence under the United States, or from discharging any duties thereof; or to induce by like means any officer of the United States to leave any State, district, or place, where his duties as an officer are required to be performed, or to injure him in his person or property on account of his lawful discharge of the duties of his office, or while engaged in the lawful discharge thereof, or to injure his property so as to molest, interrupt, hinder, or impede him in the discharge of his official duties;

Obstructing justice; intimidating party, witness, or juror

(2) If two or more persons in any State or Territory conspire to deter, by force, intimidation, or threat, any party or witness in any court of the United States from attending such court, or from testifying to any matter pending therein, freely, fully, and truthfully, or to injure such party or witness in his person or property on account of his having so attended or testified, or to influence the verdict, presentment, or indictment of any grand or petit juror in any such court, or to injure such juror in his person or property on account of any verdict, presentment, or indictment lawfully assented to by him, or of his being or having been such juror; or if two or more persons conspire for the purpose of impeding, hindering, obstructing, or defeating, in any manner, the due course of justice in any State or Territory, with intent to deny to any citizen the equal protection of the laws, or to injure him or his property for lawfully

enforcing, or attempting to enforce, the right of any person, or class of persons, to the equal protection of the laws;

Depriving persons of rights or privileges

(3) If two or more persons in any State or Territory conspire or go in disguise on the highway or on the premises of another, for the purpose of depriving, either directly or indirectly, any person or class of persons of the equal protection of the laws, or of equal privileges and immunities under the laws; or for the purpose of preventing or hindering the constituted authorities of any State or Territory from giving or securing to all persons without such State or Territory the equal protection of the laws; or if two or more persons conspire to prevent by force, intimidation, or threat, any citizen who is lawfully entitled to vote, from giving his support or advocacy in a legal manner, toward or in favor of the election of any lawfully qualified person as an elector for President or Vice President, or as a Member of Congress of the United States; or to injure any citizen in person or property on account of such support or advocacy; in any case of conspiracy set forth in this section, if one or more persons engaged therein do, or cause to be done, any act in furtherance of the object of such conspiracy, whereby another is injured in his person or property, or deprived of having and exercising any right or privilege of a citizen of the United States, the party so injured or deprived may have an action for the recovery of damages occasioned by such injury or deprivation, against any one or more of the conspirators.

R.S. § 1980.

§ 1986. Action for neglect to prevent

Every person who, having knowledge that any of the wrongs conspired to be done, and mentioned in section 1985 of this title, are about to be committed, and having power to prevent or aid in preventing the commission of the same, neglects or refuses so to do, if such wrongful act be committed, shall be liable to the party injured, or his legal representatives, for all damages caused by such wrongful act, which such person by reasonable diligence could have prevented; and such damages may be recovered in an action on the case; and any number of persons guilty of such wrongful neglect or refusal may be joined as defendants in the action; and if the death of any party be caused by any such wrongful act and neglect, the legal representatives of the deceased shall have such action therefor, and may recover not exceeding $5,000 damages therein, for the benefit of the widow of the deceased, if there be one, and if there be no widow, then for the benefit of the next of kin of the deceased. But no action under the provisions of this section shall be sustained which is not commenced within one year after the cause of action has accrued.

R.S. § 1981.

§ 1988. Proceedings in vindication of civil rights; attorney's fees

The jurisdiction in civil and criminal matters conferred on the district courts by the provisions of this Title, and of Title "CIVIL RIGHTS," and of Title

"CRIMES," for the protection of all persons shall be exercised and enforced in conformity with the laws of the United States, so far as such laws are suitable to carry the same into effect; but in all cases where they are not adapted to the object, or are deficient in the provisions necessary to furnish suitable remedies and punish offenses against law, the common law, as modified and changed by the constitution and statutes of the State wherein the court having jurisdiction of such civil or criminal cause is held, so far as the same is not inconsistent with the Constitution and laws of the United States, shall be extended to and govern the said courts in the trial and disposition of the cause, and, if it is of a criminal nature, in the infliction of punishment on the party found guilty. In any action or proceeding to enforce a provision of sections 1981, 1982, 1983, 1985, and 1986 of this title, title IX of Public Law 92–318, or title VI of the Civil Rights Act of 1964, the court, in its discretion, may allow the prevailing party, other than the United States, a reasonable attorney's fee as part of the costs.

R.S. § 722; Pub.L. 94–559, § 2, Oct. 19, 1976, 90 Stat. 2641; Pub.L. 96–481, Title II, § 205(c), Oct. 21, 1980, 94 Stat. 2330.

APPENDIX C

WELL-KNOWN INDIVIDUALS EDUCATED AT HOME

Educators
Frank Vandiver (Texas A & M)
Fred Terman (Stanford)

Generals
Stonewall Jackson
Robert E. Lee
Douglas MacArthur
George Patton

Inventors
Alexander Graham Bell
Thomas Edison
Cyrus McCormick
Orville and Wilbur Wright

Painters
Claude Monet
Andrew Wyeth
Jamie Wyeth

Preachers
Philipp Melanchthon
John Wesley

Scientists
George Washington Carver
Pierre Curie
Albert Einstein

U.S. Presidents
John Quincy Adams
William Henry Harrison
Abraham Lincoln
James Madison
Franklin Delano Roosevelt
George Washington
Woodrow Wilson

World Statesmen
Konrad Adenauer
Winston Churchill
Benjamin Franklin
Patrick Henry
William Penn

Writers
Hans Christian Andersen
Pearl Buck
Agatha Christie
Charles Dickens
C. S. Lewis
George Bernard Shaw
Bret Harte

Others
Charles Chaplin, actor
George Rogers Clark, explorer
Andrew Carnegie, industrialist
Sandra O'Connor, Supreme Court
  justice
John Burroughs, naturalist
Albert Schweitzer, physician,
  musician, writer
Noel Coward, playwright, composer
Tamara McKinney, World Cup skier

INDEX